MORE PRAISE FOR DIFFERENTIATED ASSESSMENT

"A wonderful contribution for any educator who wishes to meaningfully and fairly assess our ever-growing pool of diverse children left behind. Stefanakis's insight and practical advice is useful for all students but *essential* for the learning different—most especially English Language learners and learning disabled students."

> —**Carola Suárez-Orozco**, author, *Children of Immigration*, professor of
> Applied Psychology, New York University

"Evangeline Stefanakis's latest is the best book that's been written on how to meaningfully assess diverse students' learning. Educators and policymakers alike will benefit from a close reading of this important work."

> —**Tony Wagner**, co-director, Change Leadership Group, Harvard Graduate
> School of Education, author of *Change Leadership* and *The Global
> Achievement Gap*

"Stefanakis demonstrates an effective way of bridging the gap between diverse students and schools, where the entire school community—administrators, teachers, students, and parents—has an opportunity to explore counternarratives for itself and for the youths' futures."

> —**Maria E. Torres-Guzman**, professor of Bilingual/Bicultural Education,
> Columbia University

JOSSEY-BASS TEACHER

Jossey-Bass Teacher provides educators with practical knowledge and tools to create a positive and lifelong impact on student learning. We offer classroom-tested and research-based teaching resources for a variety of grade levels and subject areas. Whether you are an aspiring, new, or veteran teacher, we want to help you make every teaching day your best.

From ready-to-use classroom activities to the latest teaching framework, our value-packed books provide insightful, practical, and comprehensive materials on the topics that matter most to K–12 teachers. We hope to become your trusted source for the best ideas from the most experienced and respected experts in the field.

DIFFERENTIATED ASSESSMENT

How to Assess the Learning Potential of Every Student

EVANGELINE HARRIS STEFANAKIS

Foreword by Deborah Meier

JOSSEY-BASS
A Wiley Imprint
www.josseybass.com

Published by Jossey-Bass
A Wiley Imprint
989 Market Street, San Francisco, CA 94103-1741—www.josseybass.com

Jossey-Bass books and products are available through most bookstores. To contact Jossey-Bass directly call our Customer Care Department within the U.S. at 800-956-7739, outside the U.S. at 317-572-3986, or fax 317-572-4002.

Jossey-Bass also publishes its books in a variety of electronic formats. Some content that appears in print may not be available in electronic books.

Library of Congress Cataloging-in-Publication Data

Stefanakis, Evangeline Harris.
  Differentiated assessment: how to assess the learning potential of every student / Evangeline Harris Stefanakis; foreword by Deborah Meier.
    p. cm.
  Includes bibliographical references and index.
  ISBN 978-0-470-23081-7 (pbk.); ISBN 978-0-470-90962-1 (ebk.); ISBN 978-0-470-90963-8 (ebk.);
ISBN 978-0-470-90965-2 (ebk.)
  1. Learning ability—Testing. 2. Remedial teaching. 3. Individualized instruction. 4. Portfolios in education. I. Title.
  LB1134.S67 2011
  371.26'4—dc22
                                                                    2010032219

Printed in the United States of America

FIRST EDITION

PB Printing   10 9 8 7 6 5 4 3 2 1

ABOUT THIS BOOK

I s using a standardized test to determine an adolescent's future really what the 21st century calls for in preparing learners to be global citizens? Does the fact that many adolescents do not test well but speak two languages, can fix a computer, and earn significant money on eBay count? Is an education system that relies on paper-and-pencil tests to make the most critical judgments about students using the best 21st-century systems to assess and teach all students?

This book describes a comprehensive assessment system especially appropriate for multilingual and differentiated classrooms with large numbers of diverse adolescent students. Drawing from Multiple Intelligences theory, the approach is specifically aimed at helping teachers and leaders understand how each student learns and how best to tailor instruction to serve individual students' needs. Although the program makes use of conventional standardized tests and disability screenings, it places special importance on two approaches in particular: Student Portfolio Assessments and Personalized Learning Profiles.

The book and its corresponding DVD:

- Provide detailed guidance and practical tools for assessing a diverse array of students

- Include real-world examples of model assessment programs from numerous schools

- Explain how to integrate assessment into the instructional process

- Offer downloadable forms and helpful videos to help educators implement these practices

*This book is dedicated to the memory of Theodore Sizer,
who asked me to document new assessments
for high schools in which he felt the students
deserved ways for their teachers to see their assets.
His reminders offered me inspiration always.*

ABOUT THE AUTHOR

EVANGELINE HARRIS STEFANAKIS, Ed.D., is a Faculty Fellow in the
Provost's Office in Assessment and Evaluation and an associate professor in educational leadership and development at Boston University. Previously she was
an associate research scholar and faculty with the National Academy of Teaching Excellence at Teachers College Columbia University, where she was working
with the International and Transcultural Studies faculty to better understand learning challenges, leadership, and team building. For eleven years, previously, she
served as a faculty member at Harvard Graduate School of Education and was
a senior associate at Programs in Professional Education developing training
institutes for school and community leaders.

As a researcher, trainer, and program developer who links theory to practice,
Dr. Harris Stefanakis is currently developing leadership programs in the United
States and abroad. Her teaching and consulting experiences focus on school
reform and leadership in multilingual and international settings, most recently in
the United States, Greece, Norway, and China. As a researcher, frequent speaker,
and writer, she focuses on understanding how best to assess and teach all learners
from diverse language, learning, and cultural backgrounds.

ACKNOWLEDGMENTS

To those learners in secondary schools whose abilities shine in assessments that show their unique profiles, projects, and performances—the students of PS 188 (the Island School); IS 131 Dr. Sun Yat Son Middle School, of New York's lower East Side; Fannie Lou Freedom High School and New Day Academy of the South Bronx.

To the leaders in New York, the stars who see "abilities" in all children—Principals Dr. Barbara Slatin and her staff of PS 188, Jane Lehrach and the IS131 faculty, Nancy Mann of Fannie Lou Freedom High School and her teams, and the entire New Day Academy community of leaders.

To my colleagues at Teachers College and the National Academy of Teaching Excellence—Dr. Maria Torres Guzman, Dr. Douglas Wood, Dr. Veronica Denes, Claire Evelyn, Joanna Zampas, Ellen Scheinbach, Ellie Drago Severson, and the advisors to New York City's high schools.

To graduate students who were my team of scholars who captured these students' work—Amber Trujillo, Lou Lahana, Lauren Karp, Ruth Lopez, and Carol (Tao) Lin, from Teachers College.

To my editorial collaborators and DVD creators: Dody Riggs for editorial support on each chapter and to almost Doctor Colby Young of Boston University, who edited and helped create all parts of the DVD, I owe so much to what you taught me about getting this work done for others. To Andrew So, who authored Chapter Five, admiration for his teaching story.

Finally, to the essential characters who remind me how children are unique, intelligent, and way ahead of me in learning and thinking, my own three children, Rianna, Nikias, and Alexandros, who inspire me every day.

CONTENTS

FOREWORD

This is a book about reality-based schooling and the kind of assessment that can't be so easily manipulated as so many of the other data we are inundated with these days. Here is an approach to data that captures the real state of knowledge and skill that each student possesses and enables us to make judgments that are useful to student, family, teacher, and anyone else with the time to look and see. There is a real need for the kind of differentiation that Evangeline Harris Stefanakis writes about here. Her extraordinary work in the use of portfolios of student work as an approach to assessment and accountability is critical in order to achieve an authentic approach to the simple fact that we are all unique and the world needs our uniqueness.

I've watched over the years as she developed the work she presents in this book. We have spent many hours discussing students together as she watched them carefully to see what classroom teachers often lack the time to see: how they differ from each other, express their ideas, and respond to the classroom world. Harris Stefanakis took the idea of assessment for learning not as evidence of achievement but as a way to understand the varying ways in which such achievement displays itself and how this could be a tool for teaching and learning. It both analyzes and honors struggling students as they work and practice to achieve at a high level.

We are so accustomed to the demand for judgment that standardized tests are intended to give us that we've paid insufficient attention to the craft of diagnosis. Taking apart test scores is too often an exercise in futility. We pore over items or collections of items for meaning that they cannot offer those of us who seek to foster potential in individuals—unless that child is there to interpret for us. But the portfolios that Harris Stefanakis draws on help us see behind the work itself into the child's intention and meaning.

Too often also we see the differences among children as deficits and bemoan how they complicate our task as educators. But Harris Stefanakis quotes a New York City high school teacher who offers quite a different vision: she is discovering that "our students are the hidden treasure that we are reaching for" and that these students have too often hidden themselves as a response to timidity and safety.

This book is more important than ever before, coming at a time when we are being pushed to see children in clusters of types or categories, generally with numbers attached. New York City, like many other communities, divides its student population into groups labeled 1s, 2s, 3s, and 4s based on artificial test distinctions. Sometimes 1s are tops and sometimes 4s are, but we mistakenly think that in this labeling and categorizing, we are more accurately providing a framework for our roles as adults.

In fact, we as professional educators are wasting our time with a diagnosis that leaves the child entirely aside. We need instead to confront the reality of how people learn: those students who confuse us most, who seem most unreachable, are those we need to see as whole people. Some kids obviously present themselves in ways that easily fit into curricular frames and move along a visibly upward-moving line toward success as ranked in scores. But it's those who don't who frustrate teachers and frustrate the students themselves. They need our help (as do their families) in finding the threads that are woven together into a powerful pattern. We all seek to catch a glimpse of it, and then enlarge it and treasure it.

Modern technology, Harris Stefanakis assures me, will make this task easier. As a Luddite, I take that on faith. And I have a lot of faith in her based on mutual experiences we have undergone together. So I toss my technological timidity aside and urge readers to see how she puts her skills of old-fashioned observation, documentation, and keeping track of student learning together with new-fangled technology.

Differentiated Assessment is an important book that will be useful for elementary and secondary schools, but it is aimed above all at that most critical link between them: early adolescents. If we can do a better job at this transitional moment, we may do for children's learning curves what we haven't been able to do with Wall Street. In fact, this book should be read not only by those closest to the schoolhouse but by the policymakers and business community whose impatience with school reform often misses the qualities that tomorrow's educational system needs to embody. We can't build a better tomorrow if we aren't more clearly seeing the children as they are today.

DEBORAH MEIER

Hillsdale, New York
November 2010

INTRODUCTION

S omething happens to learners when they enter middle and high school. Their learning and our teaching seem to get out of sync, and they know more about what happens outside the daily life of classrooms than about what they learn in school. Perhaps we are not seeing how smart these students really are.

It's time for us to reconsider what it means to be "smart" and how we assess students' abilities in educational settings. Are the 21st-century learning environments we call schools designed to reveal and teach to the abilities of the learners they serve? Several critical questions plague today's educators as they strive to develop programs and policies that reach and teach every child:

1. How do we educate today's diverse population of adolescents to become tomorrow's global citizens?

2. How can research on learning and teaching help update educational assessment policies and practices?

3. How do we comprehensively assess what these individuals do know and need to know?

4. How do we "differentiate assessment" to address diverse learning abilities?

5. How does differentiated assessment lead to differentiated instruction so that schools can truly leave no child behind?

These are the essential questions that guide *Differentiated Assessment.*

ABOUT *DIFFERENTIATED ASSESSMENT*

The answer to these questions for leaders, educators, and parents is simple. Education for the 21st century requires classrooms that can personalize how we assess and teach *all* learners. We need educators who are equipped with classroom practices that include both the differentiated *assessment* and *instruction* to know more about each learner's abilities and capitalize on his or her strengths as a catalyst to learning.

This book and DVD of assessment tools, student portfolios, and resources chronicle best practices in innovation in differentiated assessment from New York public middle and high schools. Each chapter is illustrated on the accompanying DVD with cases of real students and assessment tools and strategies that support the learning of both students and their teachers.

Something happens to learners when they enter middle and high school.

The DVD included with this book contains PDFs and templates developed by educators and specialists from grades 7 through 12 to illustrate whole school models and classroom-based designs. These materials provide teachers with proven assessment strategies that will help tailor learning to adolescent students in middle and high schools.

Chapter One, *Education for the 21st Century: Diverse Students and Learning Challenges*, answers the question of how we educate today's diverse population of adolescents to become tomorrow's global citizens. It offers stories from urban classrooms and data from urban public school districts as clear evidence of the problems in current U.S. assessment policy and programs under No Child Left Behind and related legislative mandates for high-stakes testing for minority populations.

Part One of the accompanying DVD provides actual digital portfolios of diverse learners in grades 5 through 10 that demonstrate problem-solving skills evident in projects in English, math, science, and social studies, as well as other talent areas.

Chapter Two, "Differentiated Instruction Starts with Differentiated Assessments," offers teachers and leaders tools and an assessment framework for asking the key questions:

- Who are our learners?

- Are we finding all of our learners' abilities or deficits?

It's time for us to reconsider what it means to be "smart" and how we assess students' abilities in educational settings.

The chapter provides in-depth case studies of teachers' differentiated assessment systems that capture the assets their students bring to the learning environment. The book and DVD show how to create a Learner's Profile through units using reflective study and interviews focused on "All About Me" as an autobiographical project.

The DVD material for this chapter offers assessment tools for giving feedback and engaging students in critical dialogue on what they did well and what still needs work. These materials offer a collection of resources for defining assessment purposes, knowing your learners, examining performance assessment designs, and using multiple intelligence theory to design learner profiles to better understand individuals.

Chapter Three, "Differentiated Assessment in Middle Schools: A Window into Learners' Abilities," describes how a school community (the Island School in New York City) created a system of differentiated assessment over three years by applying New York State standards without standardization. The DVD materials for this chapter provide tools to bring together professional learning communities of teachers who use collaborative assessment conferences to work on classroom practices. The materials can be used to design a comprehensive schoolwide assessment system. These materials guide readers through outlining a portfolio table of contents, creating a standards-based design and rubrics, and developing rubrics for English/language arts, math, social studies, and science.

Both the chapter and DVD offer strategies and tools to differentiate assessment in curriculum that involves project-based learning. Specific strategies for middle and high school communities are described, including:

- Collaborative Assessment Conferences: Seeing the Details of Learning

- Profiles and Portfolios: The Window into Their Mind and Potential

- Reaching Every Language Learner Personally: Creating a Profile

Chapter Four, "Differentiated Assessment in High Schools: A Systemic Approach," features students and teachers of the South Bronx who experiment with differentiated assessment, beginning in the area of science and eventually covering all core subject areas. The chapter provides guidelines for leaders and teachers to understand:

- Differentiating Learners: Knowing Adults and Adolescents as a Community

- Digital Portfolios as Personal Stories: A Window in the Learner's Mind

- Guidelines for Classroom Assessment: Creating and Maintaining Portfolios

In the accompanying section of the DVD, tools for a high school classroom created at Fannie Lou Freedom High School are presented, including a Multiple

Intelligences Inventory, All About Me templates, checklists and work tags for reflection on assignments, and a monthly review to document learning over time.

Chapter Five, "Classroom Assessment with Digital Portfolios: A Teacher's Account," written by Andrew So, describes how he started from the beginning to introduce differentiated assessment into his curriculum with the group of English language learners and students with disabilities that he served. Andrew, a ninth-grade teacher at New Day Academy in the Bronx, describes the planning he did, the coaching that supported his growth, his direct instruction with students, his planning tools, and samples of guidelines he used to create differentiated assessment using portfolios as comprehensive assessment for his middle or high school classrooms in English/language arts and mathematics.

Chapter Six, in Part Three of the book, combines the whole process of differentiated assessment, instruction, and accommodation. Chapter Six materials on the accompanying DVD include specific examples of how teachers and leaders use differentiated assessment to personalize instruction based on a learner's profile, samples of student work, and reflections on the process and products of learning over time. Chapter Seven, "How Differentiated Assessment Guides Instruction," provides some voices from the field on the topic.

Part Four of the DVD includes a collection of sample lesson planning forms, unit planning tools, and portfolio development prompts for collection, selection, and reflection of student work. Samples of projects that differentiate assessment and instruction illustrate how to provide accommodations for diverse learners.

As one teacher of the year from New York City reflected on learning to differentiate assessment and instruction, she concluded:

> *Our students are the hidden treasure that we are reaching for behind the thorns; and they've hidden themselves very well behind timidity, fear, low self-esteem, failure, and sadness. It is our responsibility as educators to find the right way to assess and teach them, knowing that it needs to be personalized.*

Differentiated assessment is a learning process I know will offer you a way to see the assets in learners and find ways to use their potential. Join me in this quest to reach every individual and use students' intelligences to learn, grow, and develop. I look forward to hearing your stories of teaching, learning, and assessment in the future.

PART

I

THE CONTEXT OF LEARNING FOR TODAY AND TOMORROW

CHAPTER

EDUCATION FOR THE 21st CENTURY
Diverse Students and Learning Challenges

Advice to the U.S. President from Education Leaders

Our president has to look at how we are going to bring our school system into the 21st century.... We have been operating the most unequal educational system in the industrialized world, with dramatically different resources available to different students. At this point in the knowledge economy, what kids need to be able to do is to frame and solve their own problems, find and manage information, organize themselves in teams, and—with collaboration—tackle novel issues. We need to focus our curriculum on standards that evaluate how people can think and problem solve and invent and create and use knowledge in new ways and continue to learn independently. That means we have to change the assessments that we use. Most countries in the world that are high achieving have assessments that ask students to think and problem solve and investigate and conduct research. We are still having our kids bubble-in multiple-choice tests, which focus on recall and recognition rather than on these higher order thinking skills.

Linda Darling-Hammond

A re the 21st-century learning environments that educational leaders call schools designed to reveal and teach to the abilities of the learners they serve? Several critical questions, as Linda Darling-Hammond suggests, plague U.S. educators as they strive to develop programs and policies that reach and teach every child:

- How do we educate today's diverse population of adolescents to become tomorrow's global citizens?

- How can research on learning and teaching help update educational assessment policies and practices?

- How do we comprehensively assess what these individuals now know and will need to know?

- How do we "differentiate" assessment to address diverse learning abilities?

- How does differentiated assessment lead to differentiated instruction that will enable schools truly to leave no child behind?

These are the essential questions that guide this book, *Differentiated Assessment: How to Assess the Learning Potential of Every Student.* If we ask these questions in New York City, we may find that differentiated assessment is alive and well in today's classrooms but still rarely acknowledged as the judgment that counts. In the New York public schools, as in most U.S. schools, test scores rather than classroom work determine whether students make the grade (Harris Stefanakis, 1998b). In other words, students' test scores—not the body of work they compile at school over the years—is what counts.

Because of current testing policies, we *are* leaving children behind, including many who are potentially gifted or are English language learners or have special educational needs. Are we failing our students because we are not recognizing their abilities? Are we relying on one type of test to determine all individuals' futures, rather than on multiple assessments that reflect the diversity of the human mind? As a policymaker and educator, it saddens me to report what I have observed. Simply put, we are failing our students by using obsolete assessments that inaccurately and inadequately measure their abilities. In fact, I often doubt that students' learning abilities, those of adolescents in particular, are visible to those who teach them or to those who would presume to judge whether they are "intelligent." Therefore, in this book I will focus particularly on adolescent learners, including those who may be labeled gifted, learning disabled, or English language learners, all of whom present specific learning challenges.

The following example is from a true story that appeared on the *New York Times* op-ed page.

NEW YORK TIMES OP-ED: FAILING OUR STUDENTS!

By Evangeline Harris Stefanakis, Op-Ed Contributor
January 8, 2006

Beginning this week, New York City's fourth graders will take the state's standardized tests in reading and writing. Many people are looking forward to a repeat of last year, when the city celebrated a nearly 10 percent increase in fourth-grade reading scores. But not everyone is sharing in the anticipation.

Luis Castro, a 12-year-old from the Dominican Republic, is worried that he will not pass the test and thus be forced to repeat the fourth grade, again. Like so many over-age immigrant students at the school he attends on the Lower East Side, Luis is as tall as most seventh graders, has an incipient mustache, and is tired of being teased. Worse, he's afraid of disappointing his parents, who, like so many other immigrants, have pinned their hopes on their children.

New York City schools base their decision on whether to promote students entirely on results from the state achievement exams. But these tests, which are written for native English speakers, discriminate against those who are still learning the language.

Luis is a perfect case in point. His schoolwork shows that he has made significant progress since September and that he has met state standards in the work he has completed. But when Luis takes state tests, he is unable to quickly comprehend what he reads in English, and that hurts his performance . . . and his score.

Today, this is the judgment that counts, but the impact of this policy is hurting large numbers of intelligent children.

Even by conservative estimates, immigrant children like Luis account for close to half the student population in public schools across New York State. The same is true in many urban environments across the U.S. and internationally.

Doing well isn't simply a matter of knowing English. Standardized tests measure children's knowledge of "cognitive academic language," or the language of a highly literate population. Students in middle-class areas like the Upper East Side, the Upper West Side, Park Slope, and Riverdale are well versed in this language.

But students in Washington Heights, Corona, East Brooklyn, and other low-income, immigrant communities do not read, write, or speak [English] fluently. In most cases, neither their parents nor other adults they come in contact with speak this language to them, and yet, they are required to learn it to pass state tests and be promoted. Their test scores reflect the fact that they often must literally translate as they work, either from their native language to English, or from the version of English they speak in their minority community to cognitive academic English.

What is needed is "differentiated assessment" that looks at the learner's abilities in the context of a collection of evidence that provides information on what that child knows and is able to do. What does this mean in practice in the daily learning environment?

The solution to this problem, already used by many schools and districts in other parts of the country, is to use a student's body of work, or portfolio, as an additional means of assessment. Where standardized tests alone reveal only the language differences of students, a growing body of research shows that a combination of formal tests and informal assessments can indicate their progress. Portfolios, in particular, capture both the process and products of students' learning and reflect their multiple languages, multiple intelligences, and multiple abilities.

Perhaps even more important, an approach that includes portfolios would not only improve assessments of immigrant students, but would also help ensure that they receive a good education. Portfolios reveal what is being taught and help to ensure that teachers regularly observe and document the learning of each student.

Skeptics may ask, couldn't schools, under pressure to show progress, simply rubber-stamp portfolios regardless of quality? No, because, just as with statewide tests, there are clear, codified standards for judging portfolios. In math, for example, young children must demonstrate counting, numeration, and data-analysis skills.

But couldn't teachers or parents polish up a child's portfolio to make it look more impressive than it really is? That's probably true, just as it's true for any homework assignment, but the student would still be required to take standardized tests, which would reveal any discrepancies.

Differentiated assessment practices are growing nationally in the U.S.

Georgia, Hawaii, Tennessee, and Virginia have been among the leaders in adopting standards-based testing programs using portfolios and alternative assessments for bilingual students and those with limited English proficiency. Even though the state achievement tests are scheduled for this week, it's not too late for New York City schools to follow the lead of these states. In making their promotion decisions, individual schools can elect to use portfolios and other assessments to determine the fate of any child.

Researchers and the courts have repeatedly found that exclusively using any single assessment tool to determine the promotion or graduation of bilingual students is discriminatory. Until New York State creates a collection of formal tests and informal assessments that are truly comprehensive, ZIP codes, family income, and socioeconomic status will continue to be strong indicators of graduation and promotion rates. New York should stop sorting students along these lines and create a comprehensive system—a differentiated assessment system—that measures and celebrates the diversity of what all students know and can do.

The students' portfolios in Figures 1.1 and 1.2, on the DVD provided with this book, show the quality of the work that two students who were failing in school were able to do.

Exhibit 1.1. Purposes of Assessment

Improving Student Learning

- Making learning visible to students

- Fostering reflective learning and self-regulating

- Acknowledging and celebrating learning

- Communicating learning to families and the community

Improving Teaching

- Adjusting instruction

- Fostering reflective teaching to inform practice

- Acknowledging and celebrating teaching

- Improving the capacity of schools to reach for high standards for student achievement

Figure 1.1. Alsenio's Portfolio

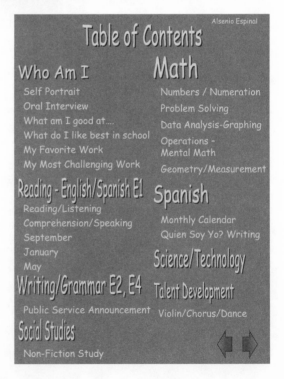

Note: The complete version is on the DVD.

Figure 1.1. (*continued*)

Figure 1.1. (*continued*)

Alsenio Espinal

My Favorite Work

My First Halloween

When I was little, about two years old, I used to love candy and I still do. But most of all, I love Snickers. I was at my grandmother's house, waiting for my cousins to get ready. My Halloween costume was a ripe pumpkin as ripe as can be. On October 31, 1994, I saw all of my cousins putting on costumes. I was scared of the one my uncle Omar had. It was some kind of mask of a hairy monster with sharp teeth. I probably didn't tell you that I only ate soft candies, like Snickers, Milky Way and so on.

Finally, everyone was ready. I was happy to leave but we still didn't. Then my cousins all showed my grandmother their costumes. First my cousin Stephanie, she was a French maid. Then my cousin Little Enrique was a pink clown. He also had a long, pink hat. Then, finally, my two twin cousins were the Disney Princesses: Marilyn and Carol. Marilyn was Cinderella with a blue gown. Carol was Belle from Beauty and the Beast and she had a yellow gown.

Table of Contents

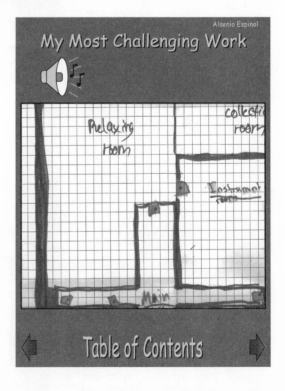

Alsenio Espinal

My Most Challenging Work

Table of Contents

Figure 1.1.   (*continued*)

Figure 1.2.   Danny's Portfolio

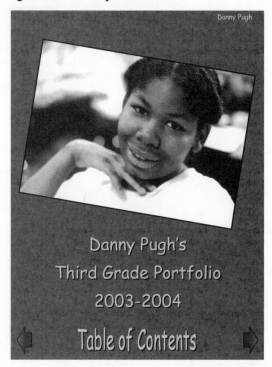

Note: The complete version is on the DVD.

Figure 1.2. (*continued*)

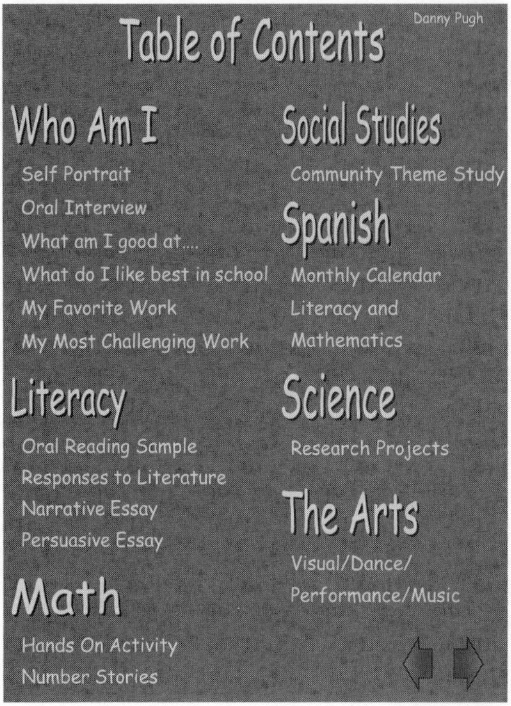

Danny Pugh

Table of Contents

Who Am I

Self Portrait
Oral Interview
What am I good at....
What do I like best in school
My Favorite Work
My Most Challenging Work

Literacy

Oral Reading Sample
Responses to Literature
Narrative Essay
Persuasive Essay

Math

Hands On Activity
Number Stories

Social Studies

Community Theme Study

Spanish

Monthly Calendar
Literacy and
Mathematics

Science

Research Projects

The Arts

Visual/Dance/
Performance/Music

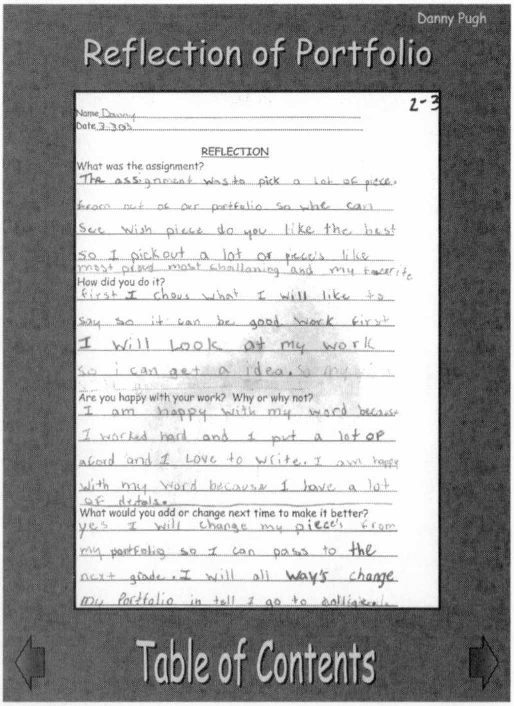

Danny Pugh

Reflection of Portfolio

Name Danny
Date 3.3.03

2-3

REFLECTION

What was the assignment?
The assignment was to pick a lot of pieces from out of our portfolio so who can see wish piece do you like the best so I pick out a lot or piece's like most proed most challaning and my facerite.

How did you do it?
first I chous what I will like to say so it can be good work first I will look at my work so i can get a idea. so my

Are you happy with your work? Why or why not?
I am happy with my word because I worked hard and i put a lot of word and I Love to write. I am happy with my word because I have a lot of detals.

What would you add or change next time to make it better?
yes I will change my piece's from my portfolio so I can pass to the next grade. I will all way's change my Portfolio in tell I go to callidge

Table of Contents

Figure 1.2. (*continued*)

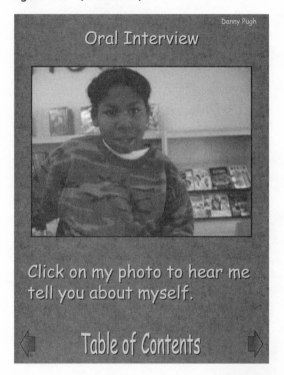

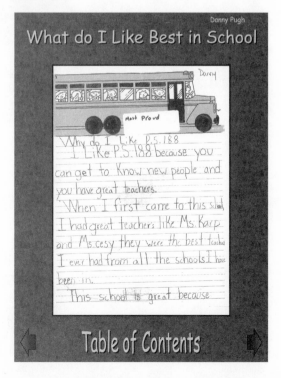

Figure 1.2. (*continued*)

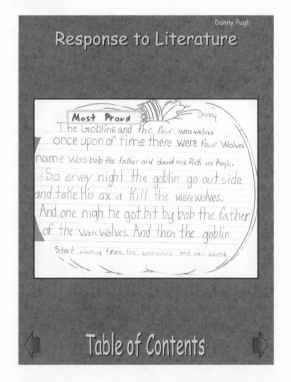

ADDRESSING THE LANDSCAPE OF ASSESSMENT POLICIES AND PRACTICE

Who are our learners? Some more examples are given in Figures 1.3 and 1.4. Are we recognizing their abilities in order to help them grow? Luis, the boy mentioned in the *New York Times* article, is not an isolated example. Current statistics from New York City's Office of Immigration show that one in five public school students is either an immigrant or the child of an immigrant. Other school systems across the United States have similar demographics, and government at all levels must establish new education policies that make it possible to provide a fair and equal education to all children.

Recent U.S. demographics indicate that the diversity of learners and the learning challenges they bring with them are astonishing. Amid this increasingly diverse student population, coupled with mandates to teach every child to high standards, education policies offer a confusing landscape. A constellation of

Recent U.S. demographics indicate that the diversity of learners and the learning challenges they bring with them are astonishing.

Figure 1.3. Who Are Our Learners? Jesus, Paz, Joyce, and Troy

Figure 1.4.   From One Student's Portfolio: "Where I Am Coming From"

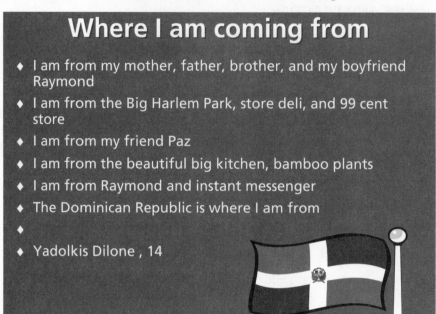

Where I am coming from

♦ I am from my mother, father, brother, and my boyfriend Raymond

♦ I am from the Big Harlem Park, store deli, and 99 cent store

♦ I am from my friend Paz

♦ I am from the beautiful big kitchen, bamboo plants

♦ I am from Raymond and instant messenger

♦ The Dominican Republic is where I am from

♦

♦ Yadolkis Dilone , 14

policies, including the No Child Left Behind Act (NCLB), the Individuals with Disabilities Education Act, and the Elementary and Secondary Education Act, all require that students who have diverse abilities, cultural differences, language differences, and learning challenges score well enough on the same standardized tests to pass grade eight, enter high school, and go on to graduate. Alternative programs for students who speak no English or have disabilities also require testing, which again may not be appropriate for students who have language issues and/or learning disabilities.

STANDARDIZED TESTING AS LANGUAGE POLICY

Kate Menken (2008) explains that the ideal behind standardized testing to measure academic achievement has translated to language policy: "An immediate effect of NCLB test policy is that English language learners are overwhelmingly failing the tests, labeled as deficient and low performing, and barred from educational advancement" (p. 35).

The current constellation of education policies is sending public schools confusing messages about whether to focus on adequate yearly progress as evaluated by test scores or to personalize teaching for individual students, many of whom are English language learners or have disabilities. As school leaders struggle to interpret these policies, large numbers of children in the nation's 21st-century classrooms are failing. So what can educators do?

The answer is simple. Education in the 21st century requires classrooms that can personalize how we assess and teach all learners. We need educators who are equipped with classroom practices that include both the differentiated assessments and the instructional skills to help them know more about each learner's abilities in languages, the arts, math, science, social skills, athletics, and other areas in order to capitalize on students' strengths as a catalyst for

> *Education in the 21st century requires classrooms that can personalize how we assess and teach all learners.*

learning. The call for differentiated instruction has been resounding for some time in schools across the U.S., but the first step in implementing this model is "to know the learners" through varied assessment formats and by using multiple ways of gathering data on individual differences. Figure 1.5 suggests that, in order to use assessment data more effectively to support the learning of students and their teachers, we need to create not a single set of tests but a comprehensive differentiated assessment system.

The remainder of this book offers ways to create such an assessment system for adolescent students in middle and high schools so that educators and community members can begin to see the learners' abilities, not their disabilities, when dealing with the challenges these students present in today's classrooms. (See Figure 1.5.)

TO SUM UP

At this time in the United States, test scores, rather than classroom work, determine whether students move on to the next grade. Students from diverse backgrounds, many of them recent immigrants whose first language is not English, are often left behind because of our existing standards. These students, including those who are potentially gifted, deserve a chance to show what they can do. Most would agree that differentiated instruction is needed to help all students learn information and skills to help them solve problems in the real world. It follows that we use differentiated assessments also.

Figure 1.5.

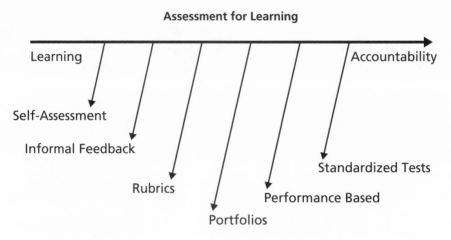

The standards we now use to evaluate these students and promote them to the next educational level are not working or relevant. A major educational priority should be to change the standardized tests we've been using for decades, which are exclusionary and keep students who know the material but are not native English speakers from being promoted. They struggle to finish the tests, translating as they go. When they have not finished within the time limit or don't understand, they are held back. Many fail a second time and tend to give up and drop out; as a consequence, their potential is not realized, and the knowledge and talents they have to offer are lost to the rest of society.

We can make our school systems relevant for students in this century by:

- Making learning meaningful to students

- Fostering reflective learning in students

- Communicating learning goals to families and the community

- Improving the capacity of schools to assess student achievement

- Changing the way our teachers view achievement

¿? DISCUSSION QUESTIONS

1. In what ways are school systems today failing students?

2. What do today's adolescents require from the education system in order to contribute to our global society?

3. Which of our educational policies and practices seem outdated?

4. How can we determine what students really need to know?

5. In what ways can our current assessment methods be updated?

6. What is differentiated assessment all about?

7. How does differentiated instruction work?

8. In what better ways can we assess what students know before deciding whether to promote them?

9. How can we go about making changes in the existing system?

CHAPTER

2

DIFFERENTIATED INSTRUCTION STARTS WITH DIFFERENTIATED ASSESSMENTS

In order to provide 21st-century learning for U.S. school-age children and offer programs that serve their diverse needs most effectively, educators first need to differentiate assessment.

The evaluation and assessment practices mandated by many U.S. education policies are too limited for the job they need to do. It is far too easy for the diverse learners in today's classrooms, especially those whose dominant language is not academic English, to fail screenings and tests and to carry the label of "failing" throughout their schooling experience. Researchers have known for years that students who are gifted or who have language or learning challenges are regularly misidentified and given special education placements. The learning differences of these children as they apply to language, the arts, or athletics are obvious to most adults, but we do not have differentiated assessment systems to help us better understand their less obvious needs and thus guarantee that all children can learn. It is not hard to imagine what Luis, the young boy in Chapter One, might say to us in light of these overlooked learning differences: "Can I ever catch on and catch up if you do not look at *all* the work I do?" New York City's mandate to use high-stakes testing as the central evaluation system to determine an adolescent's future is not unusual, even for students only twelve years old. If they fail the critical test in grade 4, grade 8, or grade 10, the consequences can be grave: they may repeat a grade, be labeled as failing or as not making Adequate Yearly Progress (AYP)—or they may not graduate from high school. Adolescents, in particular, have complex learning systems, and their abilities are often not easily understood.

A WINDOW INTO LEARNERS' ABILITIES: ADOLESCENTS WITH LEARNING CHALLENGES

Is using standardized test results to determine an adolescent's future really what the 21st century calls for in preparing learners to be global citizens? Does the fact that many adolescents in today's U.S. schools speak two languages, can fix a computer without a manual, or earn significant money on eBay have any value? Is an education system that relies on paper-and-pencil tests to make the most critical judgments about its students employing the best methods to assess and teach them? Something happens to learners when they enter middle and high school. Their learning and our teaching seem to get out of sync, and they know more about what happens outside the daily life of classrooms than about what they learn in school. Perhaps we are not seeing how smart they are. Perhaps this suggests that we reconsider what it means to be "smart" and how we assess it.

Do we pay attention to how individual students' personal abilities, not just their written work, are collected, selected, and reflected on? Do we judge students on what they can do in a variety of settings? Consider this story of an older high school student, not an English language learner but one who has spent all his school years in U.S. classrooms. No one would suggest that this all-American white student from a rural school should be left behind, but his tale is revealing:

The Poor Scholar's Soliloquy

No, I'm not very good in school. This is my second year in the seventh grade and I'm bigger and taller than the other kids are. They like me all right, though, even if I don't say much in the school room, because outside I can tell them how to do things....

I don't know why teachers don't like me. They never have much. Seems like they don't think you know anything unless you can name the book it comes out of. I've got a lot of books in my room—books like Popular Science Mechanics Encyclopedia *and the* Sears catalog—*but I don't often just sit down and read them like they make us do in school. I use my books to find something out, like whenever Mom buys anything second-hand, I look it up in the* Sears *catalog and tell her if she's getting [a good deal] or not. I can use the index in a hurry to find out the things I want.*

Could it be that the content we are asking adolescents to learn is not presented as useful knowledge? The "Poor Scholar" continues:

I guess I just can't remember names in history. Anyway, this year I've been trying to learn about trucks because my uncle owns three and he says I can drive one when I'm sixteen. I already know the horsepower and number of forward and backwards speeds of twenty-six American trucks, some of them diesels. I can spot each make a long way off. It's funny how that diesel works. I started to tell my teacher about it last Wednesday in science class when the pump we were using to make a vacuum in a bell jar got hot, but she said that she did not see what a diesel engine had to do with our experiment of air pressure, so I just kept still. The kids seemed interested, though, because it seemed like a good question. I took four of them around to my uncle's garage after school and we saw the mechanic, Gus, tearing a big diesel truck down. Boy, does he know his stuff—and it seems like science to me.

I am not very good at geography either. They call it economic geography this year. We've been studying exports of Chile all week, but I could not tell you what they are. Maybe the reason is I had to miss school yesterday because my uncle took me and his big trailer truck downstate 200 miles and we brought almost ten tons of stock to the Chicago market.

He told me where we were going and I had to figure out the highways to take and also the mileage. He didn't do anything but drive and turn where I told him. Was that fun! I sat with a map on my lap and told him to turn south or southeast or in some other direction. We made seven stops and drove over 500 miles round trip. I am figuring out what his oil cost and also the wear and tear on his trick—he calls it depreciation—so we will see how much we made.

Ironically, grave concern has been raised about the math and science skills of U.S. adolescents, especially since they do not score well on international tests. The problem is said to be rooted in the students' or the teachers' lack of ability, not in the approach to learning.

Here is the sad ending from the "Poor Scholar's Soliloquy":

I don't do well in school arithmetic, either. Seems I just can't keep my mind on the problems. We had one the other day like this: "If a 57-foot telephone pole falls across a center of a highway so that 17–3/6 feet extend from one side and 14–6/17 feet extend from the other, how wide is the highway?" That seems to me like an awfully silly way to get the width of a highway. I did not even try to answer it because it did not say whether the pole had fallen straight across the road or at an angle . . . .

Dad says that I can quit school when I am 16 and I am sort of anxious to because there are lots of things I want to learn how to do and my uncle says that I am not getting any younger. I really wonder why no one thinks I could be smarter if school was a different place [Corey, 1944].

The "Poor Scholar's Soliloquy" reveals a good deal about high school classrooms, courses, and content. Is it really that this student is not smart and is unable to pass the courses, get the grades, or earn the diploma? If we believe that intelligence is only something we can measure on an IQ test or by scores on other standardized tests, we may find we have many students who are "not smart enough" to do well in school. Could we be working with an obsolete model of intelligence that sorts students into smart and not smart without ever considering *how* they are smart?

Could we be working with an obsolete model of intelligence that sorts students into smart and not smart without ever considering how they are smart?

Teachers and other school leaders often decide who is smart and not so smart based on a few limited notions of what intelligence looks like, as echoed in the Poor Learner's story. Given what we know about Gardner's (1983) theory of multiple intelligences (see Exhibit 2.1), wouldn't this boy be considered smart, based on his particular learning profile? What about his demonstrated abilities: visual, spatial, mathematical, logical, and interpersonal intelligence? He can read maps, calculate budgets, raise animals, describe how a diesel engine runs and its relationship to physics, yet he is headed to becoming a school dropout!

EXHIBIT 2.1
THE EIGHT INTELLIGENCES

Bodily Kinesthetic Intelligence—*dancers, athletes*

- Enables control of automatic and voluntary movements
- Involves a sense of timing; knowing when and how to act
- Includes the ability to improve physical skills through union of body and mind

Visual-Spatial Intelligence—*artists, architects, pilots*

- Includes the ability to navigate through space
- Is expressed in graphic or artistic representation and interpretations
- Often involves an active imagination

Linguistic Intelligence—*poets, journalists, speakers*

- Involves the ability to understand and order work meaning
- Is expressed through reading, writing, speaking, and listening
- Involves meta-linguistic skills, as we reflect on language when we edit writing

Mathematical Intelligence—*scientists, mathematicians, detectives*

- Is responsible for sequential reasoning, deductive thinking
- Includes the ability to do mathematical computations, find patterns, and use abstract number systems
- Is evident in scientific processes and methods

Interpersonal Intelligence—*teachers, counselors, clergy, politicians*

- Involves a sensitivity to others; used by skilled leaders
- Includes sensitivity to both verbal and nonverbal communication
- Includes the ability to entertain multiple perspectives

Intrapersonal Intelligence—*psychiatrists, philosophers, spiritual leaders*

- Is used to gain self-awareness and self-expression
- Includes one's emotional nature and expression

(Continued)

- Involves reflecting about one's thinking and learning processes
- Is the last intelligence to develop fully

Musical Intelligence—*singers, composers, listeners*

- Involves sensitivity to sound and rhythm
- Is used to recognize, imitate, and reproduce music and notation
- Is the earliest intelligence to emerge—prodigies

Naturalistic Intelligence—*farmers, gardeners, geologists*

- Involves the ability to distinguish among, classify, and use features of the environment
- Is used to better understand the living world

What happens to adolescent students who think they are not smart and therefore not cut out for school?

Who are the students in our education systems we consider "smart"? What happens to adolescent students who think they are not smart and therefore not cut out for school? What happens to them emotionally and to their future learning opportunities if they think they are not smart but perhaps have talents that adults in schools do not see? How many learners are labeled disabled when in fact they have simply stopped demonstrating their abilities in school because it is not a place where their interests or interpersonal skills are valued?

In Figure 2.1, the basics of Gardner's multiple intelligence theory are offered to suggest other ways of considering students' work and a collection of the learning abilities—not the disabilities—of adolescents.[1]

As all school leaders and teachers know, it is not easy to reach every student. In order to do so, especially in secondary school, where the complexity of what they know and how they demonstrate it increases, a change in the belief system is needed.

Consider how few learner intelligences the assessment in Exhibit 2.2 engages.

Exhibit 2.2
Traditional Assessment

Name: _____

Date: _____

Class: _____

Directions. Match the letter of the important figure in the scientific revolution to the statement that best matches them.

A. GALILEO GALIEI

B. NICOLAUS COPERNICUS

C. ISAAC NEWTON

D. RENÉ DESCARTES

E. ANTOINE LAVOISIER

F. SIR FRANCIS BACON

G. JOHANNES KEPLER

1. "I feel that you can learn about the universe using LOGIC. I am famous for the statement 'I think therefore I am.'" _____

2. "I learned, through math, that the planets orbit the sun in an elliptical shape." _____

3. "I discovered the laws of motion and also invented Calculus and the law of gravity!" _____

4. "The church was angry with me because I discovered spots on the sun. I went blind making my discovery." _____

5. "I argued for people to use the scientific method to discover things rather than simply using logic. I called this the INDUCTIVE method.

_____

Written Response. Using two scientists, describe the changes the scientific revolution created. Remember to use specific examples!!! Use the back of this sheet.

Figure 2.1. Performance Assessment

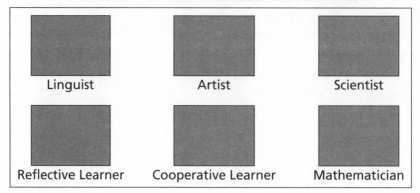

In the words of leadership gurus Bolman and Deal (1994), asking serious questions about a system that is sorting learners into haves and have-nots in terms of intelligence, despite recent research confirming that there are multiple intelligences, requires a shift in political leadership.

According to Gardner's theory, the education world needs to dramatically shift the way it thinks about learning and how we assess learners. Education leaders can begin by proposing a change in how teachers view learners and their learning potential. For example, instead of asking, "Is this a smart student?" a teacher can ask, "How is this student smart?" More important, educators may need to acknowledge that a student could "be smart" if only they were taught more effectively and in a variety of ways. Teachers need to question why a student is doing well in some classes and not in others. For the most part, I have observed that struggling learners' less obvious or nonacademic talents are seldom revealed or acknowledged in school. Even if they are, they may work against a student, as in the example of the Poor Scholar. If "education for all" truly means that no children should be left behind, then applying multiple intelligence theory to teaching learning and assessment is critical to helping school leaders and teachers program and teach all students more effectively, including those who may be difficult to reach.

THE DEMOGRAPHIC LANDSCAPE OF ASSESSMENT POLICIES AND PRACTICE

Luis's experience in a New York school is not an isolated example. Currently, one in five public school students in the United States is either an immigrant

ENGLISH LANGUAGE LEARNERS' HIGH SCHOOL PARTICIPATION

The New York City Department of Education (2006) reports an annual enrollment of 1,055,986 students, with 42 percent speaking a language other than English, yet:

- Only 33.2 percent of English language learners (ELLs) passed the English Regent Exams, compared with 77.9 percent of all students who took the exam and passed.

- For Math Regents, the ELLs' citywide pass rate is 55.5 percent compared with an overall pass rate of 81.5 percent.

- From 1999 to 2005 the dropout rate for ELLs increased from 16.5 percent to 30.5 percent, whereas the dropout rate for English speakers is 16 percent, and has not changed in six years.

Source: New York City Department of Education (2006).

or the child of an immigrant. Demographic research indicates that the diversity of learners and the accompanying learning challenges are astounding and are changing rapidly nationwide, as shown in the sidebar above.

Researchers have known for years that many adolescents in general, and English language learners in particular, are regularly misidentified for special education placement and that once a referral is made, the likelihood of testing is high. Once testing takes place,

> *Teachers need to question why a student is doing well in some classes and not in others.*

strong gravitational forces move the student toward a special education placement. Genevieve Fedoruk (1990), author of numerous studies in the 1980s and 1990s, describes U.S. child deficit model policies very clearly: "Once a linguistic minority student is referred for testing, the same student is placed in special education about 85 percent of the time. Once the student is placed in special education, despite a mistaken assessment, it takes on average six years to get out" (p. 86). Furthermore, researchers have long agreed that standardized testing done in the context of a learner's deficit model—that is, looking for deficiencies in a learner's abilities—may do more harm than good, especially for students with language and learning challenges (Harris Stefanakis, 2003). Learners may be temporarily overwhelmed by difficulties or blocked in their expression, but that does not mean that they cannot be helped to develop their strengths. As Anne Martin stated so poignantly in a 1988 article, "Predicting failure can be a way to ensure it."

Nevertheless, federal law mandates that all students, including those with language and learning challenges, be screened for special needs before they enter school, despite the fact that the standardized screening tests are often culturally biased, outdated, or both. In Boston, for example, the Early Screening Test Inventory (ESI) is used to screen all children despite its considerable limitations. Originally developed using a population of seven hundred white middle-class children from Rhode Island, the ESI had no minorities in its sample and, according to the test manual, the reliability and validity studies were done in 1972!

It is unreasonable to ask whether policymakers in U.S. school districts check the manuals of the tests they mandate to see how and when the reliability and validity studies were done, on what populations, and how recently they were last revised. Moreover, shouldn't they ask the companies that sell the tests whether they are revised annually and with comprehensive psychometric safeguards? How many school leaders and policymakers ever ask these questions?

If we use a singe test rather than a comprehensive differentiated assessment system to determine the future of 21st-century learners, how can educators assess the learners who have a combination of language and learning challenges? How can learners be assessed in ways that help them develop strengths rather than labeling them as having deficits? The first step involves looking carefully at the interaction between teacher and learner, then redefining the purposes, formats, and processes associated with the assessment of diverse language learners.

Demographic data clearly show that schools are educating an increasingly diverse student population, as well as increasing numbers of students with disabilities, with limited English proficiency, and with inconsistent schooling histories. Unfortunately, standardized tests cannot effectively do the job they are meant to do without a differentiated assessment system. The traditional psychometric models of formal assessment used to evaluate all learners consist of standardized tests and other fixed techniques that do in fact diagnose language and learning needs and issues. However, these tools assume that the deficit is in the learner.

This model is in contrast to a sociocultural approach, which argues that every learner is uniquely different and complex, and that understanding difference—not labeling the deficit—is the role of educational assessment.

A sociocultural perspective assumes that individuals learn language in real-life situations that depend on social interactions, and that these individuals display different knowledge and use various languages that depend on the social contexts in which they are learning and living. In addition, a sociocultural perspective rests on three premises:

- The languages an individual knows are a cognitive asset that enhance thinking and learning.

- Sociocultural factors affect learning; therefore, the learning context is key to understanding language use.

- Language proficiency and individual learning abilities should be assessed in context and over time.

A DIFFERENTIATED ASSESSMENT SYSTEM: A SOCIOCULTURAL APPROACH

Within the sociocultural framework, differentiated assessment is classroom-based and involves an interactive process in which teachers sit beside learners to assess and teach them. This approach realigns the usual power relationship between the dominant teacher and the dominated learner. Sitting beside each other requires the learner and the teacher to make eye contact, look together at the work created by the student, and begin a dialogue about what was done, how it was done, and what each can learn through shared reflection. What the teachers do and what students do during learning activities are examined simultaneously rather than in isolation. (See Figure 2.2.)

Differentiated assessment involves a four-step process in which the teacher:

1. Assesses and researches learners' languages and cultures;

2. Assesses the language demands of the classroom and the learning content;

3. Probes to uncover individuals' learning strengths; and

4. Gathers data on individuals by monitoring their daily interactions in various groups inside the classroom.

Figure 2.2. Sociocultural Assessment Process

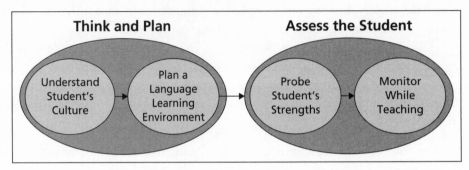

Differentiated assessment means thinking and planning, as well as:

1. Assessing individuals using portfolios to create learner profiles;

2. Assessing individuals and their work in groups; and

3. Using a sociocultural approach to examine student work.

Differentiated assessment suggests that educators look not only at what is "wrong" with the learners, but what is wrong with what they know about language and culture and the learning environment itself (the school, classroom, or curriculum) using a process to think and plan to assess students considering key issues that may play a role in what they see. Exhibits 2.3 and 2.4 give some of the issues.

Exhibit 2.3 Think and Plan to Assess

 Understand Issues of Language and Culture

- Show you value language learners

- Research students' cultural and linguistic background

- Acknowledge cultural issues in child rearing

- Recognize transitions/offer support

 Create a Language Learning Environment

- Organize the physical space for interactions

- Use symbols to translate classroom interactions

- Provide routines in schedules

- Build links to assessments/curriculum

Exhibit 2.4 Assess the Student

 Probe for Strengths/Informal Assessment

- Observe social interactions

- Question students

- Interview students

- Develop portfolios of student work

 Monitor Individuals While Teaching

- Observe language/literacy

- Analyze learning processes

- Reflect on student work using observations/portfolio

- Create a mental file on each student

The next step in a sociocultural approach to assessment is to assess the student, looking at what they do as an individual and as a member of a group of learners.

A comprehensive assessment system that includes tests, portfolios, observations, interviews, and other ways of collecting data can offer educators information to see the abilities in adolescent learners. Overall, this assessment system (see Figure 2.3) offers teachers a way to examine a learner's complex social and cultural background (who the learner is and how he or she learns); political factors (how the learner reacts in a particular environment or setting); linguistic factors (how the learner uses his or her native language and others); and academic factors (how a learner performs on a given task).

A COMPREHENSIVE ASSESSMENT SYSTEM IN A HIGH SCHOOL IN THE BRONX

Nancy Mann, principal of the Fannie Lou Hamer Freedom High School in the New York City borough of the Bronx, suggests that differentiated assessment means having a collection of information about a learner before making a decision about how best to teach him or her. As an educational leader, Mann has created a comprehensive, research-based differentiated assessment system that enables her to deal with the diverse students in her learning environment.[2] For example, at Fannie Lou Hamer they use both the New York Regents exam and portfolios to show what students know and are able to do. This creates a system for assessing how the school is doing and also how each student is doing.

Figure 2.3. Information About the Student

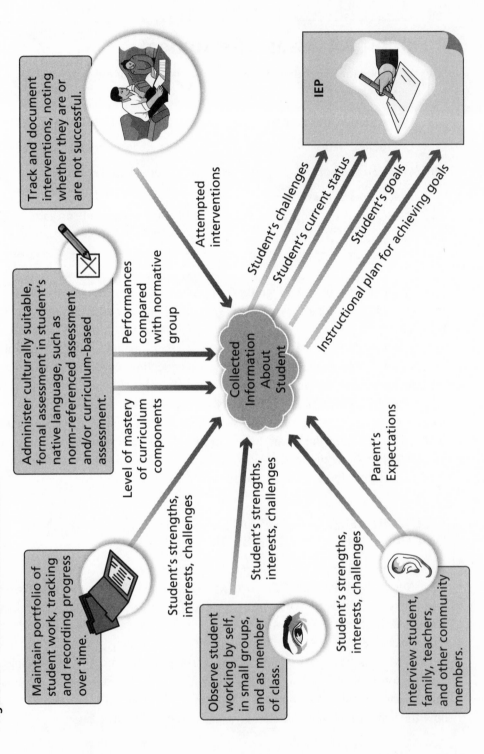

When the head of the science department, Molly, goes to the principal with questions about a student—let's say Edgar—Mann asks to see the work in his portfolio. Leader and teacher then sit beside one another to look at Edgar's work to see where his assets lie and how to use them in each school setting. In sum, the differentiated assessment—using multiple pieces of evidence to see what the learner knows—shows what he can do across many domains of intelligence. As part of her leadership role, Mann directs her teachers to identify each student's assets in order to decide how to teach them most effectively, which sends a message that all students can learn and that it is the teacher's job to make sure students do so. Yet she also "sits beside" her teachers, discussing with them what they can do together to help Edgar, as well as all other students, learn and grow.

How would this work? Look at Edgar's portfolio (Figure 2.4), and let's begin the process of making his learning visible. The portfolio provides a total learning profile and documents his growth over time, as evident in his fall and spring science exhibits. We see Edgar as a student with multiple intelligences.

As we look at this portfolio of Edgar's science exhibit, we see one excerpt that helps show his competency in documenting his work on a heart-rate lab. He shows in writing, in images, with animation, and with personal examples that he understands what a heart rate is, how it can be applied to members of his class to collect data, how it can be applied in real life—even to the point of tracing a group's heart rate during a marathon. He discusses what he did, how he did it, and what he learned from this one fall project. The remainder of his science portfolio includes other entries from his spring work, as noted on his cover page.

School leaders across the United States are faced with the challenge of meeting students' individual needs at the same time school policies are telling them to sort students into groups. A differentiated assessment system allows students to show project work, artwork, written work, presentations, etc.—all of which help show their abilities and indicate more about their multiple intelligences.

TO SUM UP

In order to provide children with programs that serve their needs effectively, educators first must differentiate assessment. The learning differences of children are obvious to most adults, but we still do not use differentiated assessment systems to help us understand their needs and achievements.

When children enter middle school, their learning and our teaching seem to get out of sync. They may know a lot about how to survive in the world,

Figure 2.4. Edgar's Portfolio

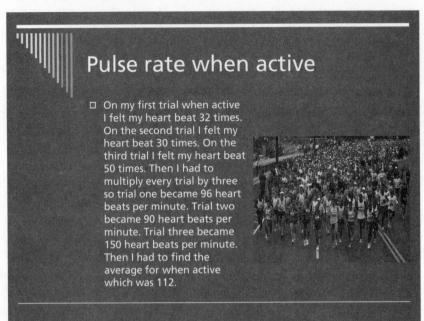

Pulse rate when active

- On my first trial when active I felt my heart beat 32 times. On the second trial I felt my heart beat 30 times. On the third trial I felt my heart beat 50 times. Then I had to multiply every trial by three so trial one became 96 heart beats per minute. Trial two became 90 heart beats per minute. Trial three became 150 heart beats per minute. Then I had to find the average for when active which was 112.

My Results

- My at rest pulse rate average was 73 and my active pulse rate was 112. That means after exercising my pulse rate increased by 39 heart beats which is a 53% increase. On the class data we did the mean, median and mode for the at rest and active pulse rate. The average for the class at rest pulse rate was 69.44 and the average for active pulse rate was 100.68. For the class data after exercising the pulse rate increase by 31.24 heart beats. I made two histogram for the class-data one for the at rest and one for the active. The graph shows how many people got the same pulse rate.

Figure 2.4. (*continued*)

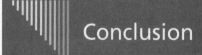

Conclusion

Homeostasis is how your body maintains balance within. Pulse rate helps maintain balance because it pumps fresh blood through the body and gives you the energy called ATP needed for activities. The two goals of the circulation system is to pump fresh oxygenated blood through the body and get rid of waste which is carbon dioxide. The heart is like the engine of the circulatory system it is divided in two four chamber. The right side of the heart pumps poor blood to the lungs. The side of the heart is responsible for pumping oxygenated blood to the body. When you are exercising the part of the circulation that increases is the heart beat. The heart pumps faster because it is trying to maintain balance by providing oxygen and getting rid of waste.

Conclusion continued

Muscle fatigue is when you are exercising and lactic acid builds up because you are not getting enough oxygen. The connection between pulse rate and muscle fatigue is that when we were squeezing the clothespin our heart started to beat faster so that the body can regain homeostasis. I think that if a person pulse rate continues to increase indefinitely he would not suffer from muscle fatigue because the heart is doing its job twice as fast. I think that our results for active pulse rate would have came out different if we went to the gym and played basketball instead of walking in the back of the classroom.

but little about what's taught in the classroom. Concern is often raised about students' math and science skills, and schools are graded on the improvements they can show in those scores, ignoring the skills students do use in their lives. Our model of intelligence may be obsolete.

Given what we know about multiple intelligences from the writings of Gardner and others, we should be able to assess students on their abilities rather than just what they can parrot back to us. Each student demonstrates what he or she knows in multiple ways—if we are paying attention. Teachers must figure out why a student is doing well in some areas, but poorly in others and address those areas. Teachers can learn ways to engage the diverse intelligences of students, helping each to learn the material in his or her own way and to feel better about himself or herself.

Educators must recognize that students who are turned off or mislabeled by the system are less likely to play the roles they could in society. Disaffected students who become discouraged and drop out of school are less likely to make positive contributions to society. We must find ways to play to their strengths by employing a sociocultural perspective that:

- Assesses language proficiency in context

- Assesses the language demands of the classroom and learning content

- Probes to uncover students' learning strengths

- Gathers data by monitoring student interactions within the classroom

¿? DISCUSSION QUESTIONS

1. Are standardized tests the best way to evaluate learners' preparation to become global citizens? Why or why not?

2. Are paper-and-pencil tests the best way to make critical judgments about students? Why or why not?

3. How can we judge students on what they can do in a variety of settings?

4. In what context do adolescents learn best?

5. How can we measure students' intelligence in more meaningful ways?

6. What happens when students accept our labeling them as failures?

7. List some ways to engage each of Gardner's eight intelligences in the classroom:

    - Bodily kinesthetic
    - Visual-spatial
    - Linguistic
    - Mathematical
    - Interpersonal
    - Intrapersonal
    - Musical
    - Naturalistic

8. How can learners be assessed in ways that help them develop strengths rather than labeling them as having deficits?

9. In what ways can teachers get to know students as individuals?

10. On what nontraditional areas would you want to assess students?

NOTES

1. A complete discussion of Gardner's multiple intelligence theory and its application in classroom assessment practices can be found in Harris Stefanakis (2003).

2. For school data reports on Fannie Lou Hamer High School, see http://schools.nyc .gov/SchoolPortals/12/X682/AboutUs/Statistics/default.htm.

II

CASE STUDIES OF DIFFERENTIATED ASSESSMENT

CHAPTER

3

DIFFERENTIATED ASSESSMENT IN MIDDLE SCHOOLS

A Window into Learners' Abilities

Multiple entry points to multiple ways of knowing and acting in the world mean that we no longer dare to measure learning in a single way. How can the diverse ways that individuals learn be understood most clearly? Language and dance, math and music, archeology and architecture, science and the arts—these "languages" that are often captured in portfolios express in myriad ways the human condition and the universe of ideas and possibilities.

We must always respect the power of language learning (oral and written, and in many different tongues) as an essential human skill in both technical terms (tests) and in expressive terms (portfolios of student work).

Barbara Slatin, school principal

CASE STUDIES IN DEVELOPING DIFFERENTIATED ASSESSMENT

This chapter describes how two New York City public secondary schools and their faculties developed differentiated assessment systems based on both standardized testing and digital portfolios over a three-year period. The journeys these school communities took in order to accommodate learners' diverse abilities offer lessons for educators on how to create whole schools and classrooms that are able to identify student needs, and then to track interventions that address them.

We no longer dare to measure learning in a single way.

As Barbara Slatin, principal of IS 188, so aptly described:

> *If you look at poor, linguistic minority, or LD students whose opportunity to learn has been inconsistent, then test scores tell you what they do not know but offer no solutions for what to do [to change it]. We need answers based on what diverse language learners can do. We need to look for students' assets, not their deficits! Given the mandates of [the] Leave No Child Behind [act], we need assessment strategies that help us intervene with those most needy students who are being left behind.*
>
> *Classrooms that differentiate assessment by using portfolios to collect and reflect on student work biweekly offer a means for teachers to see real evidence of whether students are learning, and to do something if they are not. Portfolios directly informed the dual-language instruction in all our classrooms, in both English and in Spanish. Eventually portfolios helped all students, teachers, and parents focus on improvement made daily on their language-based assignments. Teachers finally saw, in students' work, what they could do to really help.*

In this chapter, I lay out a road map for differentiated assessment describing the following parts of the process of implementation: (1) schoolwide assessment conversations, (2) schoolwide collaborative practice groups, and (3) classroom-based practices. This includes a comprehensive assessment framework designed for schools and classrooms that is compatible with the push for greater accountability and standards-based reform, but which uses multiple assessments rather than a single set of tests. I describe a set of practices these groups used as guidelines to build and sustain an assessment for a learning culture. These educators teach us that evaluations of linguistic minority students using differentiated assessment show improved results on test scores and in daily classroom work. This occurs when both teacher and students regularly assess their learning, using digital portfolios to make learning visible and to focus on observing, documenting, and keeping track of learners' skills and abilities.

A key element to keep in mind is the notion of assessment as sitting beside the learner, of having teachers, specialists, and parents regularly look at student work to see evidence of growth in literacy, numeracy, science, and social studies. This is the first step to differentiating assessment for diverse learners in order to see their varied abilities and truly work to "leave no child behind."

GRANT AS CATALYST: A COMMUNITY DESIGNS A SYSTEM OF DIFFERENTIATED ASSESSMENT

How do school communities that want to develop differentiated assessment systems begin the process, especially if most of their students and families are poor immigrants with inconsistent schooling? To directly address the need for effective differentiated assessment and instruction, principal Barbara Slatin authored a Federal Language Assistance Program (FLAP) grant to promote a differentiated assessment system for her school and its partner schools.[1] She proposed using digital portfolios and language instruction based on multiple intelligence theory (MI) for two of the most prominent language groups on the Lower East Side—Dominicans and Chinese (see Table 3.1). The following excerpt, taken from the grant proposal, defines the schools' collective goals and specifically outlines what the teams of New York City school leaders and Teachers College researchers set out to do:

This project, funded by the Department of Education in Washington, D.C., involved action research on implementing portfolio assessment in two public schools in New York, with the goal of simultaneously improving student learning and teachers' teaching. These school communities had a strong need to find new ways to find student's assets and to document their abilities in non-traditional ways so that both adults and children would benefit from innovative practices.

As a Federal Language Assistance Program, the project's goals were:

1. *To provide a comprehensive differentiated assessment system of [formal + informal assessments] for these schools to inform and personalize their instructional practices*
2. *To create a prototype for a comprehensive assessment system by adding dual language portfolios (Spanish and Chinese) to middle and high school programs and carefully monitoring student learning on a weekly basis*

Middle school principals Barbara Slatin and Jane Lenhrach faced a dilemma shared by many urban secondary school leaders whose schools had large numbers of poor linguistic minority students who scored 1s and 2s on state tests.

TABLE 3.1. DESCRIPTION OF THE TWO SCHOOLS

Characteristic Data	IS 188, Island Middle School	IS 131, Dr. Sun Yun Pak School
Population	669 students Dominican, East Indian	469 students Mixed: Chinese, East Indian, Dominican
Free or reduced-price lunch	98 percent	99 percent
Faculty	12 full-time, 14 part-time	21 full-time, 19 part-time
Program	Grades K–5 and 6–8, two schools	Grades 5–8
Achievement data		
Principal/leadership	Barbara Slatin	Jane Lenhrach

Source: New York State Department of Education.

They clearly needed a new, differentiated assessment intervention to address their students' diverse needs. They decided that as a classroom assessment system, portfolios put both students and teachers under a microscope for a period of time to ensure that focused individualized interventions would be developed and sustained, and that the products of these efforts could be archived or burned onto CDs and DVDs. These leaders and their communities agreed that digital portfolios, along with the standardized testing system, could provide individualized instructional learning plans, keep track of at-risk students' language learning, and offer visual evidence of individuals' growth and improvement. The portfolios simultaneously kept track of teachers' work and provided concrete evidence of the interventions they were implementing to reach students with combined language and learning challenges.

LEADERS' LESSONS: LOOKING AT STUDENTS' WORK MAKES LEARNING VISIBLE

Principals Slatin and Lenhrach suggested that without portfolios to make the daily work of classroom activities visible—what students do and what teachers teach—we could not track how students were learning and teachers were addressing their individual needs. As Lenhrach noted:

The drive toward standardized testing has required education leaders, research-ers, and practitioners to find ways to learn from both tests and portfolios, and thus to develop a comprehensive assessment system in which accountability is demonstrated at many levels of student achievement.

Figure 3.1 depicts the system these school communities devised to combine formal, informal, and classroom assessments with portfolios. Their basic goal was to develop a comprehensive assessment system linked to New York State standards that could track individual student achievement in more consistent ways. This would allow stakeholders to improve student learning and teachers' instruction by using test scores to indicate which students needed interventions and using portfolios to track the interventions using differentiated assessment and instructional strategies.

BUILDING A COLLABORATIVE CULTURE: KEY PRACTICES STRUCTURE ASSESSMENT CONVERSATIONS

How did educators in these challenging middle schools work together to design and differentiate their assessment system? To achieve this goal, leaders and teachers regularly sat beside each other to look at student work. The teachers used students' work samples collected over three months to discuss ways to

Figure 3.1. Using Assessment as an Intervention for Student Learning

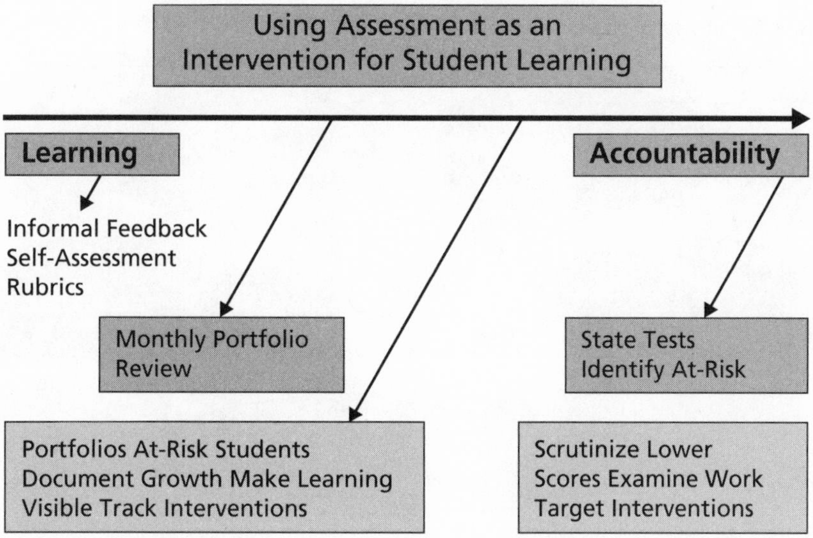

collectively find the best methods for teaching to students' assets and to address learning challenges. *(The DVD shows a sample of teacher-led groups looking at student work using protocols to address an individual student's learning needs.)*

A set of key practices (Seidel, 1997) guided the differentiated assessment redesign and implementation at these two schools, which allowed educators to focus on gaining a better understanding of their diverse students and how they learn.[2] As depicted in Figure 3.2, groups met biweekly to look at student work and carefully assess at-risk individuals' learning needs. Based on what students' classroom products revealed, they were able to work together to "leave no child behind."

> *Based on what students' classroom products revealed, they were able to work together to "leave no child behind."*

The key practices involved convening collaborative assessment groups the first week of each month, during which faculty teams looked at their students' work in portfolios and used protocols to structure their conversations. These collaborative assessment groups focused on the case studies of struggling students, and teachers practiced looking at student work to judge their abilities and consider new instructional approaches to address specific learning needs.

This approach allowed teachers to create learning profiles for students who needed more systematic assessment and instructional intervention.

Figure 3.2. Study Groups: The Key Practices

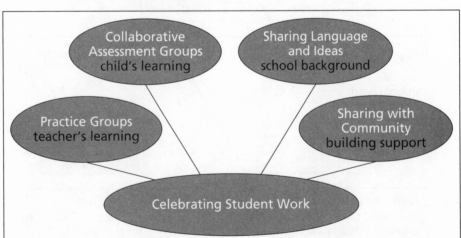

PROTOCOL FOR COLLABORATIVE ASSESSMENT

WHAT DID YOU DO?

    (Describe what is evident on paper, no judgment.)

HOW DID YOU DO IT?

    (Offer details about the subject, the format, the work, the assignment, and so forth.)

WHAT DID YOU LEARN?

    (What are the next steps in teaching this student?)

Following the key practices, teams of teachers convened classroom practice groups the second week of each month to assess how their students were learning, which strategies were working, and to outline next steps in teaching. The middle and high schools adapted the key practices to fit their schedules, using staff meetings, common planning time, or after-school sessions to have structured conversations about designing differentiated assessments that were classroom based. Principals and supervisors attended these sessions, where each teacher presented his or her students' work and asked the group to offer suggestions for next steps in teaching.

In the third week of each month, during "language and ideas" sessions, the whole faculty of each school gathered to make design and logistical decisions. They discussed implementing digital portfolios at each grade level and decided what samples of student work they would include. They linked their choices to state standards for each subject area (English language arts, Spanish, Chinese, or ESL). Every class in the school used a specific dedicated time for portfolios—20 to 30 minutes each Friday—during which teachers guided students to collect, select, and reflect on their language-development work. They made weekly assessments of student growth, choosing work samples to demonstrate that improvement was taking place. Students and teachers chose the samples they were most proud of or had found most challenging. As principal Jane Lenhrach noted in an interview:

> The quality of schooling shows in the quality of its students' work, so that if all my teachers and students are regularly examining the products from their classroom interactions for evidence of improvement in language learning, then high-quality teaching takes place.

Assessments Develop Critical Thinking and Expressive Language

These schoolwide portfolio practices provided a developmental framework for elementary, middle, and secondary schools that ensured the central focus was on students' language and learning development for every grade level or subject area. Teams of teachers responsible for all subject areas developed identical protocols for student reflection. This provided a consistent set of prompts for students to compare over time to help them improve vocabulary, language learning, and written expression, as shown in Exhibit 3.1.

Teams of teachers responsible for all subject areas developed identical protocols for student reflection.

Exhibit 3.1. Templates of New York State Standards for Collection, Selection, Reflection

**ORAL LANGUAGE SAMPLE
WHO AM I INTERVIEW**

1. What is your name?

2. How old are you?

3. Tell me about where you live.

4. Tell me about your family.

5. What is your favorite TV show? Why?

6. What is your favorite food? Why?

7. What do you like to do at school?

8. What do you like to do when you are not at school?

9. What are you good at in school?

10. What is difficult for you at school?

11. Who is your favorite person?

12. If you had a million dollars, what would you do?

13. Is there anything else you want to tell me?

2005-6
Autobiography
All About Me

My picture

Personal Statement

If I had 3 wishes, I would want:

WISH 1 _____
Because
_____
_____

WISH 2 _____
Because
_____
_____

WISH 3 _____
Because
_____
_____

Things I am Good At:
_____
_____
_____

This is My Family

My family members

_____

_____

_____

_____

_____

_____

The first year of professional development involved the following sequence of activities:

Project Timeline

Focus Areas for Year I (2005)

Fall 2005: Introduce Portfolio Development into dual-language programs and build on current assessment and instruction and practice at IS 188 and IS 131.

- Implementing Portfolio Key Practices/Classroom Workshop structure
- Focusing on Portfolio Development → Writing and Conferring → Group Share
- Conducting two formal walkthroughs of portfolios using new technologies
- Designing standards-based template for contents of portfolio to improve the teaching of reading, writing, mathematics (management, structure, and craft)
- Managing the collection of, selection of, and reflection on student work
- Documenting evidence of student language learning and teachers' teaching
- Sharing all "assessment strategies" in sessions of language and ideas with parent community

Spring 2006: Spanish and English Language Arts Portfolio Assessments

- Developing language-based teaching of reading strategies during Focus Lessons
- Developing the vocabulary program/architecture of the Reading/Writing Workshop
- Working with students to assess their portfolios, reflect on personal goals to teach dual-language reading and writing strategies
- Differentiating instruction in small group instruction through Guided Reading/Guided Literature Group lessons
- Administering and analyzing New York State Assessments/DRA and QRI-3 results to inform instruction and to provide a safety net structure

DIFFERENTIATED ASSESSMENT GUIDES INSTRUCTION: PORTFOLIO RUBRICS AS COMMON CRITERIA

From her vantage point as a school leader, principal Barbara Slatin described her school's experience:

> One of the critical elements of any system of differentiated assessment that strives to improve language and learning is feedback—the continuous loop of response to and reflection on student thinking, language, and work in progress. We found that it is possible to use rubrics and scoring systems with selected work samples from our language portfolios (tapes, writing, projects, etc.). From our school's experience, I believe that the power in differentiated assessment is using portfolios, which makes visible evidence of student learning and personalization of assessment through the descriptive processes that capture an individual student's thinking, language development, and performance at many stages.

Working with other secondary teachers from IS 131, Rosa Ng, a team leader, developed model rubrics for selected assignments in language arts and mathematics that corresponded to New York State standards, which her team used to score portfolios. The community's criteria was consolidated in a public rubric, which outlined what students needed to know and be able to do in order to graduate. The rubrics set a standard for the quality of student work and helped stakeholders assess what good work would look like to a diverse group of judges (teachers, community members, parents, and others; see the rubrics in Exhibit 3.2).

One of the critical elements of any system of differentiated assessment that strives to improve language and learning is feedback.

School leaders and teachers agree that using rubrics for portfolio assignments is helpful because they establish specific assessment criteria and provide clarity about the standards set at many levels—state, school, classroom. Rubrics, like an assessment "accordion," can guide teachers and students to reflect on performances at many levels as they relate to standards, personal goals, and individual progress. Rubrics help a school knit together accountability and assessment for learning purposes, simultaneously looking at the individual students' and the system's needs.

Exhibit 3.2. IS-131 Rubrics for Grades 7 and 8

Graduation Rubric

Student: _____

Panelist: _____

	How it looks	How you talk	How you write	Thinking about work	Specialness	What it's all about
	Aesthetics	**Oral Communication**	**Written Communication**	**Reflection**	**Creativity / Originality**	**Content**
	Neatness Organization Adornment Clarity Care taken	Clear, loud voice Eye contact Appropriate word usage Decisiveness Engaging	Grammar/punctuation Spelling Paragraphing and flow Word choice/phrasing Style/voice	Relevence Personal growth Connections Empathy Change in thought	Takes chances Unique approach Goes beyond Original work Personal stamp	Detail Complexity Accuracy Intraconnections Informative
Math Project	Novice Apprentice Practitioner Expert	Novice Apprentice Practitioner Expert	Novice Apprentice Practitioner Expert	Novice Apprentice Practitioner Expert	Novice Apprentice Practitioner Expert	Novice Apprentice Practitioner Expert

Comments _____

Science Project	Novice Apprentice Practitioner Expert	Novice Apprentice Practitioner Expert	Novice Apprentice Practitioner Expert	Novice Apprentice Practitioner Expert	Novice Apprentice Practitioner Expert	Novice Apprentice Practitioner Expert

Comments _____

Research Project	Novice Apprentice Practitioner Expert	Novice Apprentice Practitioner Expert	Novice Apprentice Practitioner Expert	Novice Apprentice Practitioner Expert	Novice Apprentice Practitioner Expert	Novice Apprentice Practitioner Expert

Comments _____

Autobiography	Novice Apprentice Practitioner Expert	Novice Apprentice Practitioner Expert	Novice Apprentice Practitioner Expert	Novice Apprentice Practitioner Expert	Novice Apprentice Practitioner Expert	Novice Apprentice Practitioner Expert

Comments _____

Copyright 2002 by Evangeline Harris Stefanakis from *Multiple Intelligences and Portfolios*. Portsmouth, NH: Heinemann.

Differentiated Assessment: How to Assess the Learning Potential of Every Student. Copyright © 2011 by John Wiley & Sons, Inc.

Middle Schools' Rigorous Standards Using Rubrics in a Learning Community

New York City public middle schools require eighth-grade students to engage in long-term projects in the major subject areas (humanities, math, and science) and to develop organizational and "executive function" skills through increasingly independent work, complete with an accountability system in their scoring rubrics. These rubrics and the portfolio presentations have created a culture of high standards, which provides students meaningful and rigorous feedback from parents, teachers, and community members. At the middle school level, especially with students who scored 1s and 2s on state tests, portfolios have become a way to showcase their language learning and provide evidence that they have achieved state standards in alternate ways. The examples in Figures 3.3 and 3.4 show how Yvette's and Billy's portfolios became a way to determine whether they needed to be retained in grade 7.

Figure 3.3. Yvette's Portfolio, Abridged

Note: A complete version of the portfolio is on the DVD.

Figure 3.3. (*continued*)

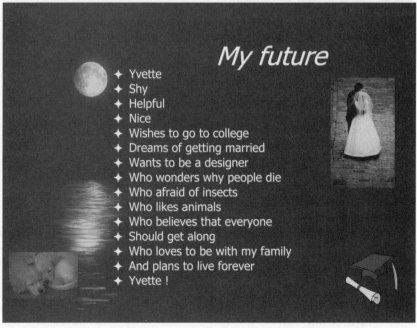

Figure 3.3. (*continued*)

Figure 3.4. Billy's Portfolio, Abridged

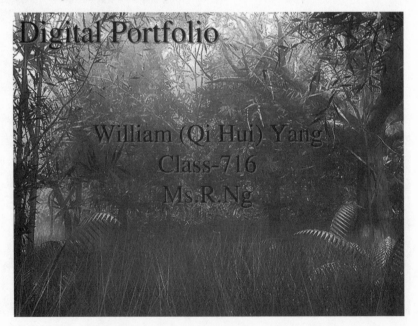

Note: A complete version of the portfolio is on the DVD.

Figure 3.4. (*continued*)

Figure 3.4. (*continued*)

Digital Portfolio Goals

I will show all the work I did on this portfolio. And then when other people see it they will know that I work hard on it. Most of the subject from this portfolio is essay. These essay is about the true experience in my live.

I wish to improve every subject in school at end of this year. Then get a high grade on report card. I will show it to my parent and so they will be proud of me.

I will keep this portfolio forever and keep as the memory in M.S.131. When I read it I will remember the things I did in this school.

Figure 3.4. (*continued*)

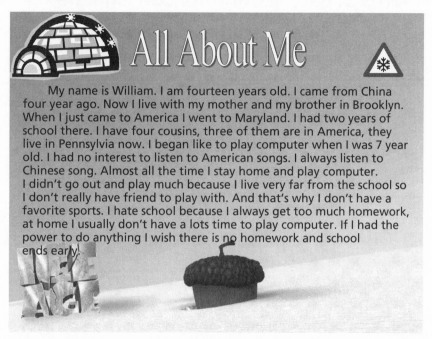

> ## All About Me
>
> My name is William. I am fourteen years old. I came from China four year ago. Now I live with my mother and my brother in Brooklyn. When I just came to America I went to Maryland. I had two years of school there. I have four cousins, three of them are in America, they live in Pennsylvia now. I began like to play computer when I was 7 year old. I had no interest to listen to American songs. I always listen to Chinese song. Almost all the time I stay home and play computer. I didn't go out and play much because I live very far from the school so I don't really have friend to play with. And that's why I don't have a favorite sports. I hate school because I always get too much homework, at home I usually don't have a lots time to play computer. If I had the power to do anything I wish there is no homework and school ends early.

INSTITUTIONALIZE PORTFOLIOS FOR GRADING AND CONFERENCES: CELEBRATING STUDENT WORK

Parents, students, and teachers hold quarterly portfolio celebrations in these two schools in conjunction with parent conferences, which allows them to set goals, using the format shown in Exhibit 3.3.

Exhibit 3.3. Parent Conference Template

Conference Goals

Student: Grade: Date:

Present at conference:
    Teachers:

    Parents/guardians:

    Other:

Portfolio Work Observations:

GOALS	The student will...	The family will...	The teachers will...

Additional notes, reminders, and/or suggestions:

Copyright 2002 by Evangeline Harris Stefanakis from *Multiple Intelligences and Portfolios.*
Portsmouth, NH: Heinemann.

Curriculum exhibitions and portfolio celebrations have become cherished rituals to celebrate the culmination of students' performance and teachers' work. The adults enjoy students' portfolio presentations, which make their academic improvement visible to their families and to the wider community. Teacher Ruth Lopez describes how she assesses and then compares work samples from Tamara's (Figure 3.5) and Luis's portfolios (in Chapter One), which demonstrate these learners' wide range of abilities as expressed within a single classroom. She summarizes the clarity this brings to her understanding of individual differences in the students she teaches:

> *For educators like myself, at the Island School and at IS 131, the notion of sitting beside the language learner, sitting beside one's colleagues, and sitting beside the multilingual families we serve is the powerful connector that allows human learning to be visible from multiple perspectives, which are shared in our students' digital portfolios.*

LEADERS' STORIES: IDENTIFYING THE ASSETS OF DIVERSE GROUPS OF LANGUAGE LEARNERS

Following middle school students' portfolios over the course of a year chronicles language learning through the selection of specific pieces. This is followed by weekly reflection on these work samples, based on a consistent set of questions:

- How was this piece done?
- What do you like best about this piece of work?
- If you did it again, what would you change?
- What did you learn from doing this work?

The school communities outlined lessons they learned at the two schools, as shown below:

I. Create assessment for learning culture in a school with a shared vision
- A professional community talks about what is possible for all adults and all children.
- Multiple intelligences (MI) theory is embodied and implemented in school practices in a learning community.

- Acknowledging that students are smart in different ways becomes part of a school's vision.

- A community combines high standards and learning, and teaches to diversity.

II. Become a school that teaches diverse language learners using multiple intelligences theory

- Portfolios of student work provide evidence that all students learn in different ways.

- Leaders, teachers, and parents use portfolios to see the diverse capabilities of all learners.

- Portfolios are individualized; student work provides evidence and data to document achievements.

III. Document learning: Portfolios for every student across the grades

- Start to implement portfolios slowly: SSS means start slowly and small.

- Initially just collect student work; select an array of work using MI as an analytic tool.

- Select work based on state standards as evidence of growth and diverse capabilities.

- Reflect on collections of student work monthly and on the learning process.

- Compile a template and a system to manage student work in reasonable ways.

IV. Develop and adapt a framework and support for portfolios

- Develop a culture of structured conversations focused on student learning.

- Consider a set of key practices for multiple audiences.

- Document and celebrate portfolios and projects with parents and the community.

- Design and develop rubrics with exhibitions and project-based learning.

Figure 3.5.   Tamara's Portfolio, Abridged

Note: A complete version of the portfolio is on the DVD.

Figure 3.5. (*continued*)

Figure 3.5. (*continued*)

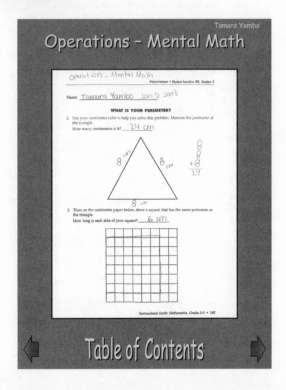

TEACHERS IN MIDDLE SCHOOL CREATE CLASSROOM ASSESSMENT SYSTEMS: SETTING STANDARDS

New York City middle school teachers Ruth Lopez and Rosa Ng, who have students whose skills range from the elementary to the middle school level in one class, indicate how differentiated assessments play a vital role in helping them take stock of how students achieve, based on state standards. Both teachers agree that looking at student work and asking questions about how to best teach diverse language learners helps them build an inclusive classroom. Simply put, there is no one way to differentiate assessment or do portfolios at the classroom level. The beauty of portfolio assessment is that it can be designed to suit the context of each community or school. Although different secondary school teachers involved in this project applied MI theory and portfolios, they had common practices—the "Three Ps"—as recurring themes and lessons learned:

1. Personalize the assessment process by collecting student work.
   - Use portfolios to create MI profiles of individual learners' strengths.
   - Assess students by sitting beside them regularly to review their work.
   - Look at student work and listen to what students say about it.
   - Help students reflect on what they do, how they do it, and what they learn.
   - Look at student work to see who the learner is as a linguist, scientist, mathematician, cooperative learner, and reflective learner.

2. Pluralize the activities offered in the curriculum with multiple entry points.
   - Redesign the curriculum using MI as a framework to note the interests of students and teachers.
   - Use MI as a lens through which to assess the classroom learning environment.
   - Pluralize the strategies used in most assignments or projects by including art, music, kinesthetic, and interpersonal activities.

3. Problem solve and brainstorm about how to assess and teach all students most effectively by looking at work samples.
   - Solve problems using collaborative assessment and conversations about student work.
   - Solve problems using student work in classroom practice groups as a guide to understanding students with bilingual or special educational needs, and adapt the curriculum and assessments accordingly.

The beauty of portfolio assessment is that it can be designed to suit the context of each community or school. At the heart of this process is the group of teachers who bring their own intelligence, high standards, and commitment to make language learning prosper and who differentiate assessment by getting to know their learners well in order to teach them most effectively. According to principals Slatin and Lenhrach, their teachers agreed that the following basic principles helped guide them to engage in assessment reform because it gave them ways to respect individual differences and use them as assets in learning:

- All learners have at least eight intelligences, which provide multiple entry points for learning, not ways to label student abilities.

- Each individual has a unique profile, based on all of the multiple intelligences; areas of strength can be capitalized on to address areas of weakness.

- Multiple intelligence theory is an analytic tool to help educators assess and teach all students and to reach more individuals more effectively.

TEACHER'S CLASSROOM ASSESSMENT IS BASED ON "SITTING BESIDE" THE LANGUAGE LEARNER

Assessing an individual within the MI framework requires teachers to reconsider the definition of assessment. The word *assess* comes from the Latin *assidere,* which means "to sit beside"; thus assessing a student literally means to sit beside him or her to examine what he or she does more carefully. I believe that this position—beside a learner—is the best way for a teacher to understand an individual, collect his or her work, assess what he or she does and what he or she needs to learn, and then to create a profile using MI theory as an analytic tool. Teacher Ruth Lopez describes this process as she keeps track of her students' individual progress in portfolios:

> I keep a portfolio of the students' writing, art, problem solving, projects, and other things they make. What they want to save is important. I ask them to help me select the work we keep. This to me is the data on a learner. Looking at their work and how it is made helps me see how they are smart. I observe when the English language learner is creating a piece of work and I listen to what he or she says about the work. This reflection, even if it is hard to understand, is a window into his or her language and learning abilities.

Figure 3.6. MI Theory: A Lens to Examine Student Portfolio Work

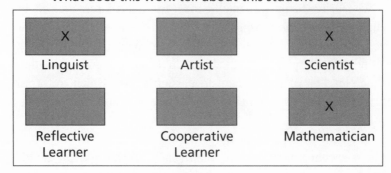

Using the MI theory as an analytic tool, Lopez looks at her students' work to see each one's strengths, whether they are mathematical, visual, spatial, linguistic, kinesthetic, musical, interpersonal, intrapersonal, or naturalistic. (See Figure 3.6.)

Teachers who, like Ruth, teach in both English and Spanish can personalize the educational process by finding ways to tap into individual learners' abilities. They do so by collecting student work over time, which may include art, problem solving, model-building, or group work. It is also important that learning activities offer students ways to do original work, so teachers create curricula that give students multiple ways to show what they know—whether through oral presentations, various art forms, writing, or performance. (See the portfolio planner in Exhibit 3.4.)

HOW PORTFOLIOS HELP TEACHERS BECOME RESEARCHERS OF INDIVIDUALS

Using the idea of sitting beside the learner as an assessment process, the teacher begins by creating the MI profile. To create the profile, the teacher needs to observe and document a collection of student work, from which he or she can then infer what each learner knows. How can this be done systematically in a classroom with a large number of students? One solution is to put some of the work back on the students' shoulders. They can collect, select, and reflect on favorite pieces of their work once a week, noting those they see as most challenging and as breakthroughs in learning. Students date their work, keep all the drafts, compile parts, and then reflect on selected pieces for 20 minutes of group portfolio time. Teachers rotate around the classroom, observing what students write and offering support for their efforts in language expression and vocabulary development. Students with writing challenges may orally record their reflections on iPods, which are then transferred to their digital portfolios.

Exhibit 3.4. Ruth's Portfolio Planner

Portfolio Planner

Name_____

Writing

	What did you choose?	Date	Reflection	Arranged
1.				
2.				
3.				

Math

	What did you choose?	Date	Reflection	Arranged
1.				
2.				
3.				

Reading

	What did you choose?	Date	Reflection	Arranged
1.				
2.				
3.				

Social Studies and Science

	What did you choose?	Date	Reflection	Arranged
1.				
2.				
3.				

Art or anything else

	What did you choose?	Date	Reflection	Arranged
1.				
2.				

Are these finished? ☐ self-portrait ☐ All About You page

PROFILES AND PORTFOLIOS: THE WINDOW INTO THE LEARNER'S MIND AND POTENTIAL

How does a classroom teacher with twenty-six students use portfolios to create MI profiles of the language learners and then personalize the learning process? Ruth Lopez and her students collected many examples of classroom activities from daily journal writing, literacy projects, shared reading record sheets, drawings, book-making, and science experiments. She started, for example, by sorting Tamara's work by date and putting a few key pieces from each quarter in chronological order. Tamara had already arranged the work for her teacher, so this was a walkthrough of her selections. Tamara then reflected on the pieces selected, as shown in Figure 3.5.

Portfolios put both students and teachers under a microscope for a period of time.

To organize how to focus only on a few students, Lopez finds that if she talks to two students a day as they walk her through their portfolios, she can infer more about the MI profiles of each of them. Using the framework in Figure 3.6, she looks at the linguistic, mathematical, visual/spatial, musical, kinesthetic, and interpersonal abilities of the individual, which help her see the variety of ways that individual students approach their tasks. Every language learner presents a picture of strength; each picture represents a unique profile of multiple intelligences.

REACHING EVERY LANGUAGE LEARNER PERSONALLY: CREATING A PROFILE

Portfolios ask teachers to take stock and to assess whether the work they ask students to do is worthwhile and is helping them gain the new skills they need. When teachers look at student work using rubrics to determine whether they are achieving to standards and how students' interests match their teaching, most students become more motivated to learn. This frequent interaction and observation of student work allows teachers and students to be co-learners, to collaboratively set goals, and to use individuals' strengths as a bridge to address weaknesses. These are the individuals whose judgments count in evaluating the power of portfolios to improve teaching and learning. As Stephanie Marshall (1992) reminds us:

Assessment is not an end in itself. It is a process that facilitates appropriate instructional decisions by providing information on two fundamental questions:

- *How are we (teacher and learner) doing?*
- *How can we (teacher and learner) do better? (p. 3)*

GOOD SEEDS GROW IN GOOD CULTURES: TEACHERS CREATE A PORTFOLIO CULTURE FOR LEARNING

Ron Edmonds (1989) reminds us in his "effective schools" research that good seeds grow in good cultures, so a key element in school improvement is to create a culture of academic excellence paired with a focus on cognitive academic language learning for the teachers involved. How do educators manage to teach all students *and* sustain this hard work?

Teams of teachers support each other in learning how to profile students in order to find better ways to teach them. The larger challenge remains how a school community can learn to nurture each individual student's language learning and each teacher's teaching style. In my earlier research (Harris Stefanakis, 1997a, 1997b, 1998a, 1998b, 1999), building on Gardner's (1983) MI theory, I concurred that "being smart" for language learners and for teachers is multifaceted, that it is not one single quality. As teacher Rosa Ng aptly stated, it is about shifting one's philosophy to differentiate assessment and instruction as a system:

It requires that we, as a community, struggle with a new way of viewing high standards in an environment that values individual differences. We are learning to seek standards, not standardization, and multiple ways of teaching and learning that personalize the process of learning two languages for students and honor their needs and strengths.

See Billy's portfolio in Figure 3.4. Listen to Rosa's analysis of Billy's portfolio on the DVD.

TO SUM UP

In this chapter, the experiences of two New York City secondary schools using portfolios for assessment are examined. The process in each case involved schoolwide assessment conversations, collaborative practice groups, and classroom-based practice sessions. School leaders agreed that digital portfolios, along with standardized tests, would provide a means to trace students' individual growth.

During the first week of the month, faculty teams determined ways student work could be structured. Teams of teachers convened classroom practice groups the second week. The whole faculty gathered during the third week to make design and logistical decisions about portfolios. After the new system began, every class in school dedicated time once a week to creating and discussing student portfolios. Finally, parents, students, and teachers held quarterly celebrations in conjunction with parent conferences. These have become cherished rituals at both schools, and both teachers profiled here agree that the experiment has been a success.

- Differentiated assessments are particularly relevant for schools in which large numbers of students score 1s and 2s on state tests.

- A critical element is finding a common rubric on which to judge the portfolios.

- Portfolios allow language learning to be chronicled throughout the year.

- Teachers bring their own intelligences and levels of commitment to the process.

- Multiple intelligences theory is an analytical tool to help educators assess and teach all students and to reach more individuals more effectively.

- Using the MI framework for assessing students requires teachers to reconsider the definition of assessment.

- Students must be involved in creating their own portfolios. If they make the decisions on what is included, the work is much more meaningful to them.

- By frequently interacting with students and observing their work, teachers become co-learners in the process.

- A key element to keep in mind is the notion of assessment as *sitting beside* the learner, of having teachers, specialists, and parents regularly look at student work to see evidence of growth in literacy, numeracy, science, and social studies.

¿? DISCUSSION QUESTIONS

1. In what ways can a classroom teacher "sit beside" learners?

2. What steps would you have to take to develop a differentiated assessment system in your school community?

3. How can educators work together to design and differentiate their assessment systems?

4. What protocols could be used to judge student work?

5. Teachers interviewed for this chapter recommend starting small. What did that involve? Why was it important?

6. What does using MI theory require of classroom teachers?

7. How can teachers profile a large number of students systematically?

8. How is it possible to make the learning process more "personal"?

9. What points could be used to convince educators to start using a portfolio system for assessment?

10. In what ways can teachers support one another in the process?

NOTES

1. The FLAP research and development design was based on earlier comprehensive school reform funding with ATLAS Communities and Harvard's Project Zero's research on multiple intelligences and portfolios conducted with the author.

2. Development of the key practices in Project Zero's work is well explained in Steve Seidel's *Portfolio Practices* (1997), a book I recommend. These key practices, with details of protocols, were outlined by Seidel and his colleagues, which for leaders and teachers has become a framework to sustain a whole school or classroom portfolio culture.

CHAPTER

4

DIFFERENTIATED ASSESSMENT IN HIGH SCHOOLS
A Systemic Approach

As a principal, I have inherited a school, started by a visionary but laden with failing learners and mostly first- and second-year teachers. Given our test scores, they are either going to fire me or close us down. We have to find new ways to see the abilities in these students and find out how to teach them.

D. Fernandez, 2007, personal communication

When I first met this strong and handsome Latina woman, I thought her tales of woe about leading an impossible urban school were an exaggeration, but after one visit I realized she was telling the truth.

Evangeline Harris Stefanakis, 2007, personal communication

WHY DIFFERENTIATE THE ASSESSMENT? A STORY OF HIGH SCHOOLS' CHALLENGES

Urban high schools often do not seem like learning environments, yet finding ways to make learning visible can offer new vision to the larger community. In the Bronx in this two-year-old high school of four hundred students, New Day Academy (NDA), the test scores were dismal, the curriculum and assessment practices were not well defined, and general chaos prevailed. Housed in two wings of an old building, students were walking the halls rather than working in their classrooms. Engaging students and teachers in learning new assessment structures seemed a tall order, yet it would be a good test of differentiated assessment as a window into the learners' abilities. As Jonathan Saphier (1993) writes, "Good seeds grow in good cultures," but in this troubled school, few seeds had ever been planted to create a learning environment for adults and children. Nevertheless, I saw the NDA as fertile ground, and I wanted to look at the leader, the teachers, and the learners simultaneously, and perhaps my words, "prepare the soil" so that a learning environment could grow.

> *"Good seeds grow in good cultures," but in this troubled school, few seeds had ever been planted to create a learning environment for adults and children.*

This small school in the Bronx was struggling to find ways to keep the adults and children focused on learning, rather than on struggling for control of the school.

The need for this pilot program at NDA was clear: standardized assessments showed that a majority of students were failing, scores on the New York Regents exam were of the worst in New York City, and few students were making adequate yearly progress. New interventions that focused on differentiated assessment and instruction were clearly warranted, as this school was desperate for a serious improvement plan.

DIFFERENTIATING LEARNERS: KNOWING THE ADULTS AND CHILDREN AS A COMMUNITY

We began the pilot assessment work as leaders by asking: Who are the learners at NDA and what are their assets?

It took only a short time to see that most of the school population, adults and children, were English and Spanish speakers from the Dominican Republic and Puerto Rico. They laughed, joked, and bantered in Spanish, but tried to do their schoolwork in English. One of the first issues to address was: How can students show what they know on standardized English tests when they are one learner with two languages, and what they know is what they can articulate in a combination of English and in Spanish? What formats can truly assess and nurture these learners' abilities?

With principal Daisy Fernandez's guidance, a team that included researchers from Columbia University's Teachers College National Academy for Excellent Teaching (NAfET) began to develop a learning culture in which portfolios were used to collect, select, and reflect on student work, and in which a differentiated assessment system could function. Two classrooms were selected to begin the process, one grade 7 and one grade 9, each with about twenty-five students. Surprisingly, both teachers, Andrew and Carl, offered to be part of this pilot project, even though they were both in their second year of teaching.

The principal and leadership team followed a trusted portfolio principle (Seidel, 1997): make sure to start slowly and small—what we referred to as SSS. As a consultant from Teachers College, I was brought in to introduce portfolio assessment to the school.

I demonstrated digital portfolios to students, showing what they look like done in PowerPoint and how they could create one. One small issue I had not anticipated was that neither the teachers nor the students had ever worked with PowerPoint. In fact, they rarely even used computers in this school, although it was the year 2007! Furthermore, there were only seven or eight laptops available in the classroom, and getting enough equipment for each student to learn on became an issue.

DIFFERENTIATED ASSESSMENT: DEVELOPING A CLASSROOM ASSESSMENT SYSTEM

Andrew's seventh-grade class was the first to have a demonstration lesson, which showed them DVDs and CDs of student portfolios from another New York City school. They asked a lot of questions and surprised their teacher by being ready to start on this work right away, saying it was "much more fun" than writing about books they had not read. As a group, we looked at samples projected on the board, talked about portfolios being collections of student work, and agreed that they would begin working on the first section, called "Who Am I?" which asked them to describe themselves. This was a section where they would all be authors and could use reflective tools, pictures, music, or art pieces they personally selected. (See Figure 4.1.)

This was the key—that the process of assessment was personalized. Each student was able to tell his or her own story, complete with a photo. They found it easy to draw, write, or find pictures to describe the best things about themselves, and it became a way to share their lives outside of school. Validation of who they are and what they bring to the learning environment was obviously very important to these students and a great way for their teachers to start to really know their learners—the first step in differentiated assessment and instruction.

> *This was the key—that the process of assessment was personalized.*

DIGITAL PORTFOLIOS INTRODUCED AS PERSONAL STORIES: WINDOWS INTO THE LEARNER'S MIND

After the demonstration lesson, the students announced that they were ready to get to work on their laptops. It was hard to keep up with them: they wanted to learn PowerPoint, colors, sounds, and animation, all within 5 minutes—and they hardly knew how to type! With two adults in the room, roaming around giving quick tutorials, these seventh graders stayed with the work for over an hour and then asked if they could stay longer.

The first task was clearly defined for each student but manageable in one period using the basics of PowerPoint templates:

> *Using a digital camera and a disc converter, each student could put his or her personal portrait into the cover of a portfolio. Uploading the picture and personalizing a cover with name, date, school, and year was the first step. Next they followed by creating a table of contents, external portfolio design based on state standards, subject area content, and project-based work.*

The issue of how to manage a group of twenty-eight students was partially solved by appointing student tutors, whom we called our Tech Team. When the students began experimenting with their laptops, it become apparent that some students were already tech savvy. It was evident that they could almost teach themselves PowerPoint, given their comfort levels with the computer. These tech-savvy students became the Tech Team. They were given extra credit for community service and cited as being community leaders by the teachers to other students. This strategy for providing the extra help we needed in technology—students helping students—was feasible and highly practical, in that students are often more nimble on the computer than their teachers or other adults. In fact, having a Tech Team of only five students helped provide the

Figure 4.1. "Who Am I?" Template

All About Me

My Picture

Date of Photo-Place-Year and Setting

This Is my Family

Members of my family

_____
_____
_____
_____
_____

Figure 4.1. (*continued*)

If I had 3 wishes, I would want:

WISH 1 _____

Because _____

_____

_____

_____

WISH 2 _____

Because _____

_____

_____

_____

WISH 3 _____

Because _____

_____

_____

_____

Things I Do Best

_____

_____

_____

_____

_____

_____

_____

My Favorites

My favorite color is _____

My favorite pet is _____

My favorite song is _____

My favorite friend is _____

My favorite TV show is _____

My favorite subject is _____

My favorite fruit is _____

My favorite food is _____

My favorite hobby is _____

My favorite sport is _____

My favorite holiday is _____

My favorite movie is _____

My favorite book is _____

necessary quick tutorial to a group of twenty-eight students, which kept everyone engaged in writing and creating the Who Am I? section of their portfolios.

Students were offered a few simple training tips to help them create their portfolios. These related to the use of PowerPoint and a digital camera, uploading and saving pictures, dating their work, and organizing folders on the "desktop" to keep their portfolios in. Each student was given a "jump drive" with his or her name on it on a key chain so that they could collect their work from various locations in and out of school. The teacher kept these jump drives so students could save work and it could be backed up in each classroom's computer, which essentially served as an archive of the classroom's work. The students' sense of ownership of their work, carefully arranged and saved on these jump drives, fascinated even the most difficult-to-manage student. Over time, getting students at this very challenging school to participate in portfolio work was never a problem with either seventh or ninth graders. As the semester continued, more students were selected by their advisory teachers to be part of the Tech Team, which became a type of honor that students coveted.

An important factor in building a culture of assessment for learning was that the principal, Ms. Fernandez, let the Tech Team students also serve as the portfolio leaders for their classes. They were able to get special help in her office from consultants so that they could create exemplary portfolios and so that she could learn how they did it. In small groups of five or six, they worked for three one-hour sessions, bringing in their work collected earlier in the year, selecting pieces they felt were worthy of their portfolios, and then writing reflections on their work. It was surprising how willing these students were to be singled out and to be called out of the classroom to work on a special project that would put them in charge of teaching their peers.

As we looked at samples of what the students created, we learned a good deal about what they were learning—and also what the teachers were teaching. Both the principal and the NAfET advisor, Ellen, noted while reviewing one class's portfolios that there was very little writing being done in one ninth-grade classroom, where the teacher was having trouble controlling students' behavior. These results showed up when students brought their portfolios to us in March; most students had included little written work, with samples dating only from January on. The principal and NAfET advisors could clearly see that an intervention to focus on adding writing to the curriculum was needed in this classroom.

On the other hand, the seventh-grade students seemed to shine when it came to collecting, selecting, and reflecting on their work using digital port-folios. An excellent example of the seventh graders' quality of work is visible in

Essence Scott's portfolio (Figure 4.2). She carefully created a table of contents, followed by the humanities, math, and Who Am I? sections of her portfolio. Surprisingly, she selected some very personal work to make public, including a humanities project in which she wrote about what it would be like to be a slave girl and be raped. The powerful metaphors she used and her choice of language revealed a lot about her knowledge of the subject and her ability to characterize the story. These seventh graders took their portfolio collections very seriously, using samples of their class work to create digital stories about themselves. For students with learning or behavioral challenges, portfolios offered an expressive outlet for them to tell their personal stories in new ways. Andrew's collection of his seventh-grade students' digital stories in Chapter Five show how digital portfolios serve as:

1. Diagnostic/teaching tool

2. Documents growth over time

3. Grading/transition tool

GUIDELINES FOR CLASSROOM ASSESSMENT: CREATING/MAINTAINING PORTFOLIOS

The best news for NDA school leaders and teachers was that students do the work to create and maintain their portfolios, and the teacher just has to schedule the time to make this happen. Teachers were surprised to learn that the creation and maintenance of digital portfolios was not difficult, once students had samples of what they could look like and a few tutorials to give them the necessary computer skills.

> *Teachers were surprised to learn that the creation and maintenance of digital portfolios was not difficult.*

Carl, a ninth-grade teacher, was having a difficult time getting students to listen to his lessons and complete assignments. While observing in his classroom, it was not uncommon to see students stand up, go over and hug a girlfriend, come back and slump in a chair, and put hats over their heads. Yet when Fernando, the "class Casanova," got a chance to create a digital portfolio that would let him tell who he is, what he thinks about, and to pick up photos from My Space, he was involved for hours at a time. Using his elementary skills in PowerPoint, which he learned in 10 minutes, he created a digital portfolio in three 45-minute sessions (see Figure 4.3). His follow-up assignment was to add work to his portfolio every two weeks, annotating his work samples with reflections on what he did, how he did it, and what he learned.

Figure 4.2. Essence's Portfolio, Abridged

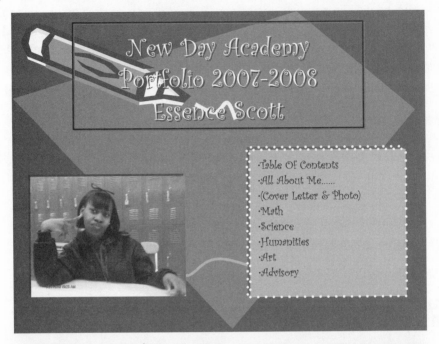

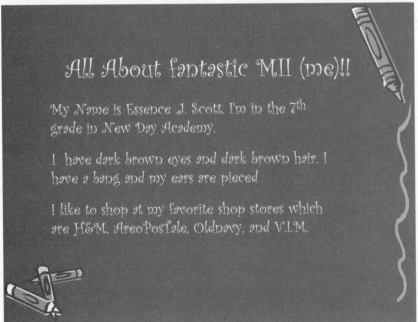

Note: A complete version of the portfolio is on the DVD.

Figure 4.2.   (*continued*)

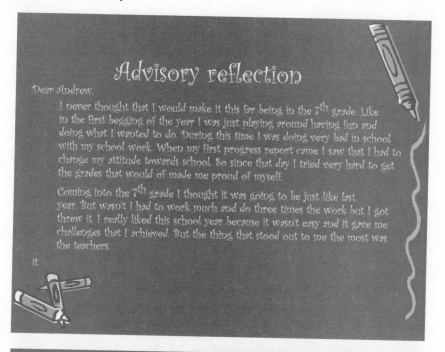

Advisory reflection

Dear Andrew,

I never thought that I would make it this far being in the 7th grade. Like in the first begging of the year I was just playing around having fun and doing what I wanted to do. During this time I was doing very bad in school with my school work. When my first progress report came I saw that I had to change my attitude towards school. So since that day I tried very hard to get the grades that would of made me proud of myself.

Coming into the 7th grade I thought it was going to be just like last year. But wasn't I had to work much and do three times the work but I got threw it. I really liked this school year because it wasn't easy and it gave me challenges that I achieved. But the thing that stood out to me the most was the teachers.

it

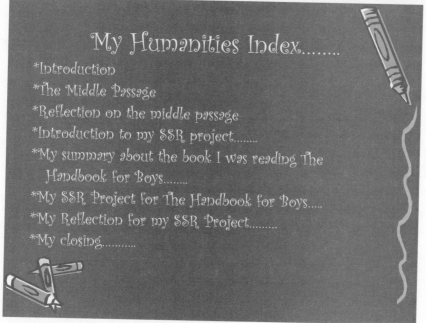

My Humanities Index........

*Introduction
*The Middle Passage
*Reflection on the middle passage
*Introduction to my SSR project.......
*My summary about the book I was reading The
   Handbook for Boys........
*My SSR Project for The Handbook for Boys.....
*My Reflection for my SSR Project........
*My closing..........

Figure 4.2. (*continued*)

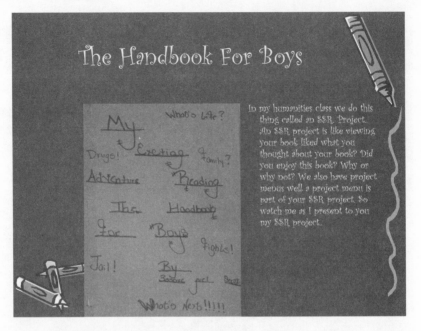

Figure 4.3. Fernando's Portfolio, Abridged

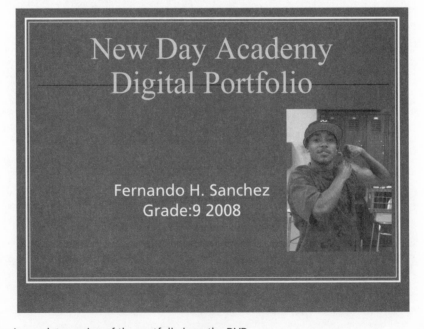

Note: A complete version of the portfolio is on the DVD.

Figure 4.3. (*continued*)

All about me

- My name is Fernando Sanchez I'm a 9th grade student at new Day Academy. The things I'm going to talk about today is what I'm good at and what I want to be when I get older.

My Family

- Hello my name is Fernando and I'm going to talk about my family. Start off with the mother the one I came out of. I love her so much I thank her for the things she did for me: for watching over me and giving birth to me. My mom is like a god and also beautiful. My mom's got a glow to her, I mean like when I'm down and I just hear her voice I'm back to the old me. I apologize for hurting you and yelling at you, I do those things cause I love you. Now my sister Christina: I love her so much I mean of course we get into it the most, I cant help it, we're getting older right but when you down know your brother here for you no matter what. Now my three brothers I love you guys like what can I do without you I love all of my brothers if I had longer arms best believe I would hug you and never let go. Last but not least my step dad Darnell yea lets go you already know I cant for get u like come on you my dad I want to thank you for being there for my mom and for her kids when we was down u gave us the energy to love each other thank u dad I love u.

Figure 4.3. (*continued*)

MY DREAM...

- Basketball is my favorite sport because I love doing team work and doing fancy moves. To me playing basketball keeps me away from the streets.

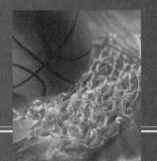

If I had 3 wishes:

- If I had three wishes I would wish for me and for my family to be happy.

- My second wish would be for me to finish high school and to go to college.

- My third wish is last but not least to be a basketball player.

Fernando's portfolio was created in May of his ninth-grade year and shows only a few pieces of class work. He spent more time documenting his progress by filling in the template of the Who Am I? section. Talking about the information he needed with two other girls, he added pictures, colors, and even animation.

It was interesting to see the contrast between Fernando's portfolio and that of his classmate, Cindy Rojas (Figure 4.4). Their portfolios show the uniqueness of their learning profiles and are one way these students were able to express their personalized learning. These beginning portfolios clearly became windows into these learners' abilities and got them excited about collecting projects, activities, and other work samples from their daily life in school.

TO SUM UP

The case study in this chapter was of a new high school in the Bronx whose test scores were dismal, curriculum and assessment practices were not well defined, and general chaos prevailed. Standardized assessments showed that the majority of students were failing, and scores on the New York Regents Exam were some of the worst in New York City.

A team, including the author and the school principal, began by assessing the learners' deficits and assets. Two classrooms, one seventh grade and one ninth grade, were selected for the pilot program. Some students learned to use PowerPoint quickly, so they were assigned to a Tech Team to assist other students.

The process and the results helped the research team learn a great deal about what students were learning and what they were interested in. For example, the team learned that one of the classrooms needed extra help in language skills. A teacher's view of this pilot project is presented in the next chapter.

- Knowing the needs of the community is important in deciding what actions to take.

- The key is to personalize the process and allow students to tell their own stories.

- Letting students help others with technology helped both students and teachers with the process.

- Students developed a great sense of ownership in their work and were never reluctant to participate.

- Teachers were surprised to learn that the creation and maintenance of digital portfolios was not difficult, once students had samples of what they could look like and a few tutorials.

Figure 4.4. Cindy's Portfolio, Abridged

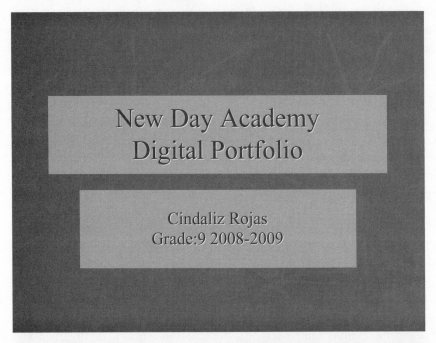

Note: A complete version of the portfolio is on the DVD.

Figure 4.4. (*continued*)

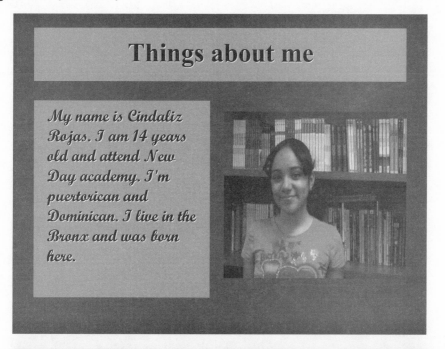

Things about me

My name is Cindaliz Rojas. I am 14 years old and attend New Day academy. I'm puertorican and Dominican. I live in the Bronx and was born here.

This is my family

My mother-Yolanda Pagan
My brother-Alex
My sisters-Jessica and chrisette Rodriguez
My father-Alejandro Rojas
Me☺

Figure 4.4. *(continued)*

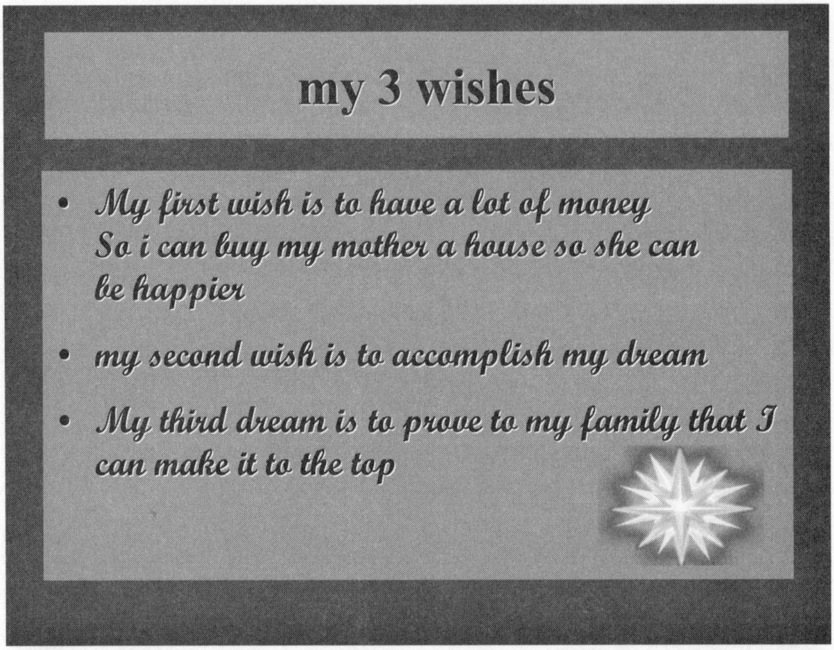

my 3 wishes

- My first wish is to have a lot of money So i can buy my mother a house so she can be happier

- my second wish is to accomplish my dream

- My third dream is to prove to my family that I can make it to the top

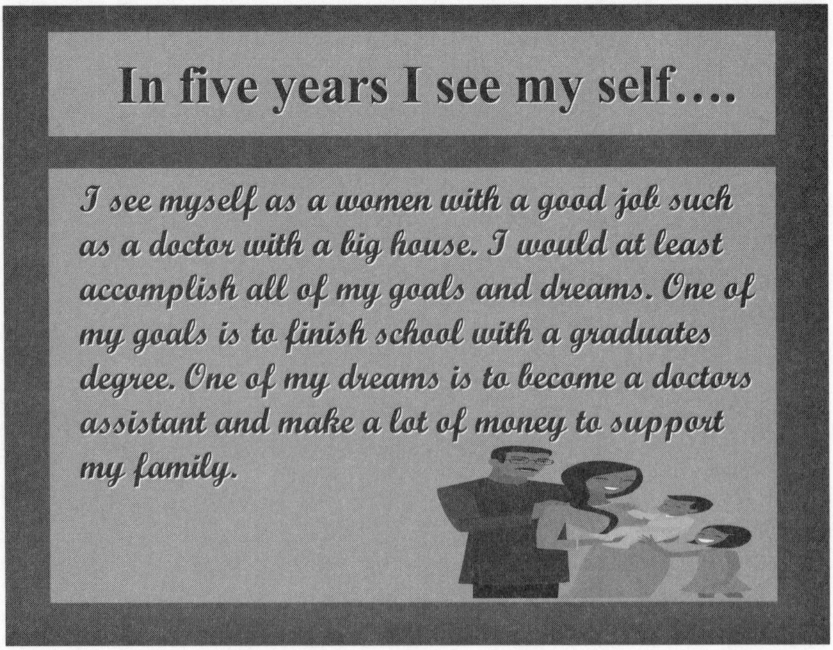

In five years I see my self....

I see myself as a women with a good job such as a doctor with a big house. I would at least accomplish all of my goals and dreams. One of my goals is to finish school with a graduates degree. One of my dreams is to become a doctors assistant and make a lot of money to support my family.

Figure 4.4. (*continued*)

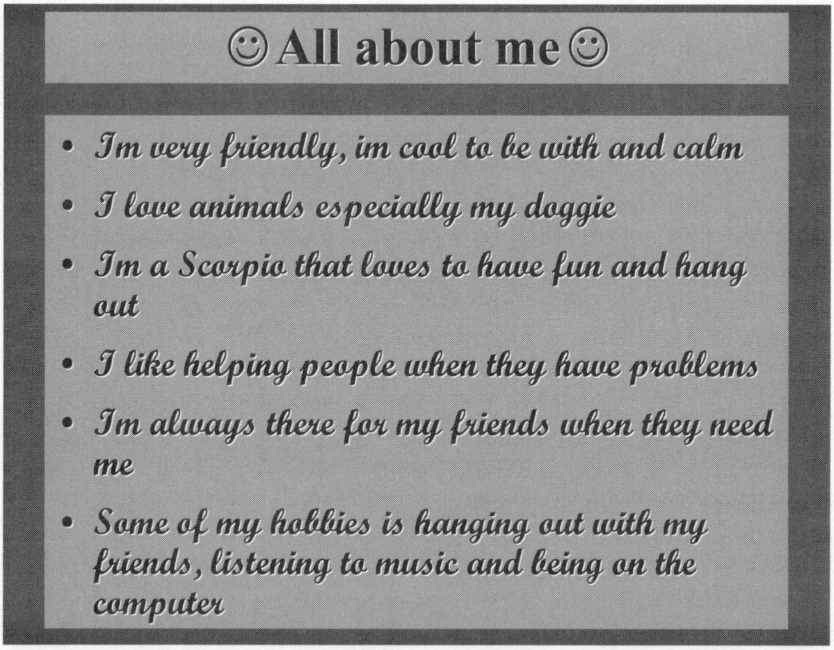

☺ **All about me** ☺

- *I'm very friendly, im cool to be with and calm*
- *I love animals especially my doggie*
- *I'm a Scorpio that loves to have fun and hang out*
- *I like helping people when they have problems*
- *I'm always there for my friends when they need me*
- *Some of my hobbies is hanging out with my friends, listening to music and being on the computer*

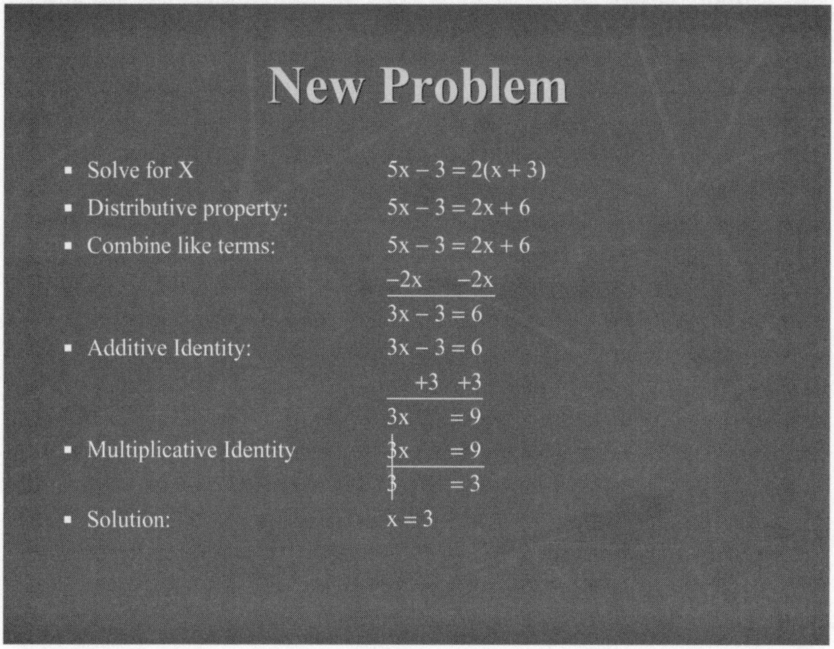

New Problem

- Solve for X $\qquad$ $5x - 3 = 2(x + 3)$
- Distributive property: $\qquad$ $5x - 3 = 2x + 6$
- Combine like terms: $\qquad$ $5x - 3 = 2x + 6$

$$\underline{-2x \quad -2x}$$
$$3x - 3 = 6$$

- Additive Identity: $\qquad$ $3x - 3 = 6$

$$\underline{+3 \quad +3}$$
$$3x \quad = 9$$

- Multiplicative Identity $\qquad$ $\dfrac{3x}{3} \quad = \dfrac{9}{3}$

- Solution: $\qquad$ $x = 3$

¿? DISCUSSION QUESTIONS

1. In this school, what sorts of problems were being addressed by developing a differentiated assessment system?

2. When students have little or no familiarity with or access to computers, what can be done?

3. How can teachers overcome the reluctance of students to "share" themselves with peers?

4. What about the process captivated students in this pilot study?

5. What ways can ownership in the process be incorporated into assessment?

6. What types of things can be learned from reading through student portfolios?

7. What did Essence and Fernando share about themselves in the portfolios in this chapter? What insights does this provide on their various intelligences?

8. In what way could their teachers use this information in the classroom?

9. What reasons does the author give for expanding the program to include all grades? How would you recommend rolling the program out?

10. What is likely to happen to the scores of these students on standardized tests?

CHAPTER

5

CLASSROOM ASSESSMENT WITH DIGITAL PORTFOLIOS

A Teacher's Account

By Andrew So, New Day Academy

Eric loaded his memory stick onto the laptop computer and navigated to his PowerPoint file, as he had done countless times before in the last three months. On a hot June day, three days before the end of the 2007–2008 school year, two fans futilely attempted to cool the seventh-grade classroom. Seated around the room were Eric's advisor (a special education and mathematics teacher), his humanities teacher, an English department coach, four of his classmates, two of his classmates' parents with younger siblings in tow, and Eric's aunt. On cue, the classroom lights dimmed, the audience quieted, and all eyes turned to blue glow projected onto the chalkboard. Eric looked expectantly at his advisor, who hit the record button on a small camcorder and nodded toward the student. Eric hesitated, took a breath, and began his portfolio presentation.

DIFFERENTIATED ASSESSMENT: SEEING THE LEARNER'S ABILITIES

Eric had been through two rocky years at New Day Academy (NDA), a small school in the South Bronx that serves students in grades 6 through 12. In sixth grade, he struggled to control his behavior, language, and impulsivity. He failed the majority of his classes, despite demonstrating high intellectual ability. Eric lived at home with no siblings and a single mother, who worked and studied full-time and had her own difficulty dealing with family and housing issues. Eric spent a lot of time away from home on his own. His appearance at school sometimes suggested poor hygiene.

At the start of his seventh-grade year, Eric hit a low point. He began the year with a new advisor, but displayed much of the same impulsive, inappropriate behavior and disengagement from class work. He also continued to have difficulty fitting in and making friends. Some classmates made fun of him and others stayed away in order to disassociate themselves from his erratic language and behavior. Two weeks into the school year, Eric stopped coming to school. He spent ten days traveling around New York City alone—riding the subway everywhere from Queens to Staten Island to Coney Island and passing time at the main branch of the New York City Public Library on Manhattan's Bryant Park—until he was picked up by truant officers on the Long Island Railroad. Upon returning to school, he said, "There is no point to seventh grade. If I don't come to school I will still go to the eighth grade." Although his views were not entirely valid, Eric made it clear that school as he knew it didn't match his needs and interests.

MAKING LEARNING VISIBLE WITH PORTFOLIOS

Eight months later, Eric stood in front of teachers, peers, and strangers to present his digital portfolio. Despite having struggled through much of the school year, Eric presented a distinguished portfolio exhibiting skills, knowledge, and creativity that had not been apparent in much of his other schoolwork. He explained how math and economic concepts could be connected through currency and exchange rates. He compared and contrasted the science behind tornadoes and hurricanes. He shared his essay on the history behind the movie *Schindler's List* and presented what he had learned about the Revolutionary War and Civil War. Eric also added a personal touch to his portfolio by uploading background images of his favorite subway trains and train stations, and by adding the video of a public service message on transit safety. He used slide transitions, bold colors and lettering, and a final scrolling credits page thanking all the staff and teachers who helped him along the way. Eric also read a three-page letter chronicling his progress during his seventh-grade year, including an honest reflection of the highs and lows, from an account of his favorite field trip to the Empire State Building to an assessment of his behavior and emotions. Following his presentation, he successfully defended his work and presentation by fielding audience questions. All the while, he demonstrated strong critical thinking, logic, reflection, and analysis by using New Day Academy's five Habits of Mind: evidence, perspective, connections, relevance, and supposition.

> *Despite having struggled through much of the school year, Eric presented a distinguished portfolio exhibiting skills, knowledge, and creativity that had not been apparent in much of his other schoolwork.*

During the process of creating his digital portfolio, Eric's relationships with his peers improved dramatically, as did his motivation in the classroom (although he still had progress to make). His technological abilities allowed him to join a small Tech Team of students who spent extra time at school working on their portfolios, learning the ins and outs of PowerPoint, and importing and editing photographs of class work. In class, Eric helped other students prepare their presentations. By the end, Eric found that this process had allowed him to show what he had learned—and to learn while working—better than anything else he had done in school thus far. No standardized test would have given him the platform on which to display not only the range of knowledge exhibited in his portfolio, but also the skills that cannot be easily quantified: oral and visual presentation, creativity, independent work, and computer and graphic skills. The digital portfolio allowed Eric to engage with his work in ways that traditional assessments did not. Eric had finally been given a chance to shine.

PORTFOLIO ASSESSMENT AT NEW DAY ACADEMY

At NDA, portfolios are used as a platform for students to provide evidence of their learning and development. The pieces presented in a student's portfolio are meant to be more than just a collection of his or her "best work." Portfolios should be project-based, relevant to the real world, and require problem-solving

> *The pieces presented in a student's portfolio are meant to be more than just a collection of his or her "best work."*

and critical-thinking skills (known at the school as Habits of Mind). Portfolios do not include assignments that require only rote skills or recall, like many tests and quizzes. Portfolios allow students to demonstrate deep understanding, rather than the broad bank of facts and skills required by many standardized tests.

Portfolio-based assessment has been one of NDA's core principles since its founding in the fall of 2005. As Eric presented his portfolio, seventy eighth-graders were preparing to become the first class promoted to high school, and a class of eleventh graders was fretting about the challenges ahead of them as NDA's first senior class. Most NDA students live in and around the local Morrisania neighborhood, statistically one of the most impoverished areas in the nation (U.S. Census Bureau, American Community Survey, 2006). The student body is split approximately fifty-fifty between African American and Hispanic students, the majority of Dominican and Puerto Rican descent. About one in five students receives some form of special education services, and 14 percent are designated English language learners. At any given time, about 5 percent of students are reported homeless or in temporary housing, with many more in some state of uncertainty.

NDA was founded to replicate East Harlem's Central Park East Secondary School (CPESS), a pioneer in the progressive small schools movement in the early 1990s—the Clinton administration recognized it as a model of urban education—and also a "portfolio school." However, its founder, Deborah Meier, wrote in the school's 1993 handbook that "CPESS [is] not meant to be copied piece by piece." This proved relevant, as the circumstances and backdrop of NDA's creation differed in a number of ways from those of its model school, not the least of which was the national and citywide emphasis on standardized testing and the need to cover the breadth of the New York State standards.

At first, New Day Academy gave little thought to preparing students for state tests, instead favoring a teacher- and student-driven exploratory curriculum. After all, in its prime, CPESS had been able to ignore Regents tests completely, thanks to a waiver from the New York State Board of Regents. But by the time NDA entered its second year in 2006, well into implementation of No Child Left Behind, the pressure on new schools to perform well on state-mandated assessments was high. At the same time, a first-time principal took over for the founding principal, who was forced to resign suddenly due to health reasons.

It also became apparent that difficulties with behavior, attendance, and student motivation were more than just first-year anomalies. NDA's culture, structure, and discipline needed to be improved in order to give its vision and philosophy a chance to be realized.

The process of building a good school and developing a school culture is no easy task. Given its student population, New Day Academy confronts a greater than normal challenge. Every school, regardless of location, has students with a range of social, emotional, behavioral, and learning needs, but like many schools in low-income and underperforming districts, NDA students

> *The process of building a good school and developing a school culture is no easy task.*

encompass the extremes of student needs. And if the challenge of meeting these disparate needs isn't enough, external forces base the success or failure of the school and its students on a set of standardized state tests administered once a year. These include English language arts and mathematics tests in grades 6 through 8, and five New York State Regents tests for high school students. New York City's controversial school progress reports for elementary and middle schools base 85 percent of a school's letter grade on student progress and performance on the two standardized test scores. (The remaining 15 percent is based on surveys of the school environment submitted by students, parents, and teachers.[1]) High school progress reports are more well-rounded, taking earned credits into account along with Regents pass rates.

Through all of this, however, portfolio-based assessment has maintained its place at the school. Although the portfolio assessment process is far from perfect (What school system is?), with each year it has grown more organized and refined, and the hard work of so many has had an impact. In fact, for the 2008–2009 school year, the New York State Board of Regents granted New Day Academy a waiver—along with twenty-seven other high schools that are part of the New York Performance Standards Consortium—for four of five Regents tests (excluding English), allowing them instead to implement Portfolio-Based Assessment Tasks as a high school graduation requirement.

NEW FACULTY GETTING STARTED WITH DIGITAL PORTFOLIOS

When I joined the New Day Academy staff as a special education teacher in the school's second year, I had little experience with teaching or learning in a portfolio system. Although my previous school, a small independent school for students with learning disabilities, was far from traditional, portfolio assessment was not part of the curriculum. I had gained some familiarity with portfolios during graduate school through research and school visits and had created my own professional portfolio Web site. I also had encountered portfolio assessment when I was a seventh- and eighth-grade student in Oregon. My classmates and I were told to select two assignments, to write a reflection on them, and place them in a folder. We only spent time discussing or thinking about the portfolios on the one or two days that our teachers asked us to select work. No presentation or defense was required, and I don't remember seeing the work again. Despite my lack of direct experience helping students create meaningful portfolios, I subscribed to the underlying educational philosophy that NDA's and CPESS's portfolio assessment was based on, particularly theme- and project-based interdisciplinary instruction, which emphasized critical thinking and problem solving in favor of rote memorization.

In the winter of 2008, with support from the National Academy for Excellent Teaching (NAfET) at Columbia University's Teachers College, the school administration decided to pilot a digital portfolio project at New Day Academy. The initial reasons for digitizing portfolios revolved around improving organization, logistics, and presentation. Digital portfolios would explicitly unite the various components of each student's portfolio into a single exhibit, they would alleviate concerns about how to store portfolios for the long term, and they would make students' work more professional and presentable.

> *The hope was that, on seeing their students' final digital portfolios, the teachers would gain the incentive they needed to participate in the next year's expanded program.*

The administration planned to pilot the project with just two advisory groups in the first year and then slowly expand the project schoolwide. Schoolwide initiatives often face resistance when they require teachers to change the way they work or to go beyond their already overwhelming responsibilities with no additional incentives; for this pilot project, the two teachers would invest themselves in the process voluntarily. Students would bring work from various classes into advisory rather than taking the digital portfolios to every class; thus, the content-area teachers did not need to buy in to the program. The hope was that, on seeing their students' final digital portfolios, the teachers would gain the incentive they needed to participate in the next year's expanded program.

Personally, I was very excited about what this opportunity offered to the students, teachers, and school. For one, having created my own professional digital portfolio a few years earlier, I knew first-hand how much more convenient and impressive a portfolio on a single, flat disc is than in a heavy, bulky binder. But most of all, I knew that any kind of work with computers would give our students the much-needed opportunity to develop greater technological proficiency while also engaging them in their work. Although students in the South Bronx love My Space and YouTube as much as any other "tween" or teen, in our school there appears to be a significant technology gap between students with predominantly low socioeconomic status and students in the middle and upper classes in other New York Public Schools. I was lucky enough to grow up in the eighties and early nineties in a family with the means to use computers at home; my dad brought home the Apple II computer when I was just beginning primary school. Through childhood and adolescence, I taught myself everything from gaming and word processing to basic web design, as well as spreadsheet, database, and graphics work. I had taught computer skills classes to New York City middle school students and worked with my students on computers enough to know what technology skills students did and did not possess. It bewildered me that, one generation later, the vast majority of students from low-income communities still cannot type at a functional rate because they don't have sufficient opportunities to use computers. I had witnessed how technology could capture the attention and imagination of children and adolescents and believed that digital portfolios would engage my students in the portfolio process and encourage them to reflect on their learning. So when given the opportunity, I didn't hesitate to volunteer myself and my seventh-grade advisory class to pilot the project. Between my class and a ninth-grade advisory class, the project had representation in both the middle and high school grades.

THE CLASS AND THE CHALLENGES

Each of the thirteen students in my advisory group had his or her own story and distinct personality, as all students do. Nine of them had returned for a second year as my advisees. Two students, Shawn and Leslie, were new to the school. Leslie, a quiet, considerate girl, was repeating seventh grade because she had achieved the lowest performance level on the math and ELA tests; after finding out Leslie was being held back, her mother transferred her to New Day Academy. Shawn, a tall, outspoken boy who was one year over age yet extremely bright, had transferred because of behavior problems and frequent fights at his previous school. Two other students had been transferred to my advisory. Christopher joined the advisory group in November when his previous advisor quit, forcing the administration to distribute the students among the remaining teachers. The second was Eric, who had been reassigned to my advisory in hope that a change might get him on track behaviorally and academically.

Nine of the students were black, five were Hispanic, one was African American and Puerto Rican. None of them was currently designated an English language learner, but two students had been previously. Jemma was born in Italy to Ghanaian parents before they moved to the Bronx to run a neighborhood store. Christina's parents had emigrated from the Dominican Republic and were primarily Spanish speaking. Her father passed away in December of that year, after which she spent a month with family in the Dominican Republic before returning to school. Six of the students were being raised by a single mother, aunt, or grandmother, and two students had parents who were in the process of separating. Each student had his or her own profile of strengths and struggles in reading, writing, and math, but unlike the schoolwide ratio, just one student was designated as having special needs. That student was not able to finish the project. Although classified with emotional disturbance, he was an excellent listener and a strong problem-solver with an excellent memory. However, he frequently got into social conflicts and had trouble focusing and writing in class. He lived with seven cousins, and his overwhelmed aunt explained that she had difficulty keeping track of him. The school's dean suspected that he was already involved with local gangs. Not long after the project began, he received a superintendent-level suspension for a serious behavioral offense.

Every student except Leslie had compiled a portfolio the previous year. Even Shawn had completed a portfolio at his last school. However, the students would soon learn that the seventh-grade portfolio process would be far more comprehensive than what they were accustomed to. The lack of complexity in sixth-grade portfolios was partly by design and partly because the assessment process was still in its early stages. The idea was that sixth graders, who needed the most support and scaffolding, compiled portfolios with less stringent requirements, but they were actually undeveloped because the staff lacked the training to help students develop adequate portfolio pieces and help them reflect on the learning process. Few of the students' portfolios were actual projects that naturally exhibited a student's critical thinking and fluency with the Habits of Mind. Many of their pieces from science, a subject that lends itself naturally to experiments and projects, were actually multiple-choice or fill-in-the-blank tests. Although the students may have been genuinely proud of their performance, a quiz or test would not display the necessary evidence of learning and progress. A system was in place for the students to reflect on their work, but the three-question reflection sheets did not probe in enough depth to develop meta-cognitive thinking or high-level reflection. At the end of the collection period, their work was presented on display boards, along with a reflective letter written to the advisory and audience (see Exhibit 5.1). Overall, their sixth-grade portfolios were just teasers compared to the challenge of the digital portfolio.

When I hinted to the students that they would begin working on a digital portfolio, they were immediately excited. With the limited technology available, being able to use the computers consistently was a privilege. PowerPoint was chosen as the platform through which students would present their work. Given the situation, PowerPoint was the logical choice: all school computers were already equipped with the software and most students had at least some experience with it. Furthermore, Internet connections were unreliable at best, so a web-based system (using blogs, Web sites, or another online storage system) was not an option. Just getting working computers was going to be a challenge. We had two laptop carts containing twenty computers each for the whole school, and at any given time only about two-thirds of them were charged and functioning properly. Our "technology coordinator" was a paraprofessional who often struggled to keep the computers organized amid his other responsibilities.

Just getting working computers was going to be a challenge.

The physical setting provided another challenge to creating an adequate work environment for the students. Just two weeks before the pilot work was set to begin, the advisory group had to change classrooms. As a special education teacher with part-time administrative responsibilities, I did not have a classroom of my own. I shared one classroom for a team-teaching class, and our "Learning Center," a resource room for students needing additional help, could only squeeze in six students. Additional classroom space was extremely limited; we already had six grades of approximately 360 students and about twenty classrooms crammed on one floor. Until January, my advisory classroom had been held in the very small teachers' lounge, with two couches, a refrigerator, and a microwave providing constant entertainment. When the lounge had to be given up to the ESL classes, we moved to the narrow counseling room—two students linking hands could touch the front and back walls. For one hour three mornings a week, the students and I had met in this tiny room to discuss issues, including character development, conflict resolution, and current events.

Exhibit 5.1.
Advisory Letter Guidelines

Portfolio Presentation—June 2008

Junior Institute, New Day Academy

These questions are designed to help you determine the content and organization of your advisory letter. You are not restricted to answering only these questions.

Date

Dear Advisor Name and Audience,

Paragraph 1—Introduction

- How has this school year been for you overall?

- How has your experience this year been similar and different from last year's?

Paragraph 2—Experiences

- What experiences, good and bad—field trips, extracurricular activities, school events, etc.—stand out to you as particularly memorable? Why?

- What have you learned from these experiences?

- Who has supported you through this year, academically and emotionally?

Paragraph 3—How You've Changed

- How have you changed and progressed as a person this year?

- How are you different now compared to how you were at the beginning of the school year?

- Did you achieve the goals you set for yourself at the beginning of the school year? Why or why not?

Paragraph 4—What You've Learned

- What are some specific things you've learned from your classes that you will remember for a long time?

- What are some things you've learned from your relationships?

- What are some things you've learned about yourself this year?

Paragraph 5—Where You Go from Here

- What are some things you need to improve on academically, behaviorally, socially, and emotionally?

- What are your goals for next year and beyond?

- How will you achieve these goals?

Paragraph 6—Conclusion

- What lessons or words of wisdom will you take away from this year?

- Who would you like to thank?

- Give any last words before you leave for the summer.

Sincerely,
Your Name

I intended that, once the process began, we would use most of the three advisory periods each week for students to compile work, reflect, revise, and digitize their portfolio pieces and digital portfolio presentations. In reality, multiple periods or parts of a period often were consumed by other matters. Sometimes important lessons and events came up, and periods occasionally were lost because the laptop computers were unavailable. This could happen because the technology coordinator was absent and no one else had the key, or because the laptop cart had unwittingly been given to another class. For the most part, however, the schedule was set and the entire advisory period was quickly consumed by portfolio work. With the first 10 minutes of class needed to set up and sign out laptops and the last five needed to return them, this actually left just 45 minutes of work time.

STUDENTS AND TEACHER AT WORK

The project officially kicked off with Dr. Harris Stefanakis's visit at the end of February. Having an outside expert come in to explain the portfolio process helped highlight the importance and uniqueness of the project. That day, students first reacted with surprise as they entered the advisory room to find an unusual guest. In a school with mostly young teachers, about half of whom were teachers of color, a tall Greek American woman with graying hair seemed to the students a most unlikely visitor, and some (to my embarrassment) were not afraid to comment on it. Soon, however, the students began to grasp the significance of her visit. That an outsider, and not only any outsider but a university professor, saw enough potential in their upcoming portfolio work to come to the South Bronx spoke volumes to the students. Dr. Harris Stefanakis modeled the type of PowerPoint presentation the students would be giving in a few months and shared examples of digital portfolio pieces from other schools. Seeing the pictures and brief bios of other middle school students immediately engaged the class, even if partly for the wrong reasons. I couldn't decide whether to sigh or laugh when each photo of a boy or girl brought a murmur of, "Oh, he's cute," or, "Take a look at her!" from students of the opposite sex.

Nevertheless, with each sample portfolio, the students were gaining a valuable mental picture of what they would be creating. Whether or not to provide students with examples when they work on open-ended assignments or assessments is not so simple a decision as it might initially seem. Some teachers fear that providing examples for assessments where creativity is an essential piece causes two problems. First, students might copy the models rather than using their own creative talents. Second, if creativity is actually a component being assessed, providing examples to a student might make it difficult to determine whether the student truly created the product independently. Despite these arguments, it is difficult to deny that good teaching must involve modeling expectations and scaffold student learning so that students have the opportunity to succeed.

From my experience, I feel that middle school students in particular need models. A majority of young adolescents, particular those in highly social settings, seem to repress their imagination and creativity because of

> *From my experience, I feel that middle school students in particular need models.*

social self-consciousness; they are afraid of showing something different from their peers for fear that anything different might be ridiculed or criticized. (Of course, the most hardened adolescents can find a reason to make fun of anything.) This stands in stark contrast to most elementary students, who will design elaborate productions that display the gamut of their vivid imaginations. With minimal guidance, elementary students will still display their creativity, while most middle school students will be paralyzed if not given clear guidelines. At the end of the educational timeline, high school students, with their increasingly developed ability for abstract and critical thinking, are more likely to be able to craft an adequate assignment with limited instruction and support. Middle school students are still developing the cognitive capacity to create a schema for how to approach an assignment. For example, to determine how to approach an assignment with minimal guidance or scaffolding, a student needs to take the perspective of the assessor, teacher, and audience to decide what they feel is most important, appropriate, and wanted. Furthermore, the work done by professionals in the real world relies on models, whether basing a legal argument on prior court rulings or planning a marketing campaign that is modeled on an earlier successful campaign. We say that we need to see what we will be creating first: a seamstress needs a pattern, a construction-site manager needs a blueprint, and a student needs a model. Given this, it was necessary to model the presentations for the students, and it would turn out that each student produced an incredibly creative portfolio. Instead of constraining the students, it expanded their imagined realm of possible presentations and provided a good starting point. Three months after viewing the examples, the students' final portfolios actually turned out to be very different in both appearance and content.

With the help of Ellen Scheinbach, a teacher coach provided through NAfET, I set up for our first advisory period following Dr. Harris Stefanakis's visit. A laptop computer was set up for each student, the teacher's laptop was projected on the screen, and samples of what their first pages might look like were displayed on the wall. Rather than addressing the portfolio pieces first, we decided to jump directly into the creation of the PowerPoint presentation. The hope was that the students were already developing their portfolio pieces in their content-area classes and that allowing them to use computers right away would generate immediate excitement for the project. Having just exhibited model portfolio presentations, it would have seemed disconnected to the students if we didn't work with presentations as well.

The first element the students worked on was the title page, table of contents, and autobiographical Who Am I? section. To encourage the students to expand their Who Am I? pages, Ellen and I gave the students writing templates that encouraged them to tell about various topics, including their family, three wishes or dreams, and a list of favorites. This was an ideal starting point for the students, since most middle school students' favorite and most accessible topic is themselves and their friends.

After the first couple of weeks, students were given free reign to edit, revise, and digitize their portfolio pieces, write reflections (including their year-end letter), and design the visual appearance of the presentation. While they were working, I would rotate among students, spending more time with those who were behind or had the most pressing needs but attempting to at least check in with all thirteen students. We also taught students how to digitize their physical work; instead of scanning it (we didn't have a scanner), students photographed the work they wanted to insert into their presentations. They learned how to alter the dimensions of a photograph in order to fit the given space and also how to record audio segments into their presentations. For example, a number of students recorded themselves introducing the portfolio and its contents to the audience. One student even managed to display a video within his presentation.

As the process progressed, a number of challenges arose. Some students started to stray off task, and the students' various levels of technological proficiency meant that every student had vastly different needs. Moreover, the portfolio pieces selected by most students required significantly more revision and reflection than I had anticipated. And, finally, as a result of these challenges and more, the pace of the project was much slower than we imagined it would be.

When students started to stray, Ellen or I would usually be able to provide individual support. But it happened at least twice that a number of students seemed to hit a wall simultaneously. Maybe they were spending too much time on a single page, continuously editing and re-editing for days, or maybe they were succumbing to social distractions that kept them from completing the work at hand. In such instances, I would pass out a progress checklist (see Exhibit 5.2), which included questions that helped students monitor what components they had completed, how much progress they had made, and what needed to be included before they finished. For many students, the checklist helped them get back on track or identify a component they had left out. Others still needed intensive individual assistance.

The students' diverse technological proficiency was expected, but that didn't make it any less difficult to address. Certain students needed explicit step-by-step instruction on technical procedures, while other students were done before I even provided instructions. For example, within the first few days, Leslie and a small, shy boy named Tyrik had already created multiple PowerPoint slides with exciting colors, pictures, and slide transitions, while the rest of the class still struggled to type words on their opening pages. Due to these differences, the idea arose to create a Tech Team made up of students who would receive additional training so that they could become peer tutors for their classmates. Supported by research on peer-assistance programs, Ellen, Dr. Harris Stefanakis, and I thought that these leadership opportunities would both empower the Tech Team members and engage all the students through peer modeling and social interaction. The Tech Team training sessions were held during school, when the students could be pulled out of other classes—as a rule, elective classes, but occasionally core courses. However, the purpose of the team was not fully realized. The sessions morphed into individualized portfolio work sessions with Ellen, Dr. Harris Stefanakis, and sometimes myself, although I often had another class to teach. When the team members returned to advisory class, they now had a wealth of new ideas gained during the work sessions. However, they used advisory time to implement the ideas on their own work rather than assisting peers who had fallen behind. I realized that peer assistance only works when the motivation to assist others outweighs another motivation, such as their own motivation to finish their own portfolios.

In retrospect, it's clear that there were two approaches we could have taken to improve the Tech Team. To develop competent peer tutors, the students would have needed more than just training in computer skills. They would have needed to be taught how to tutor and collaborate with one another, and they would have needed an additional incentive to help their classmates. We could have provided specific training on how to know when classmates needed assistance, how to ask whether classmates needed assistance, and how to interact with classmates when

Exhibit 5.2.
Digital Portfolio Progress Checklist

(Circle your response for each question.)

1. How many slides do you have so far?   1   2   3   4   5   6   or more

2. Have you added at least one picture?   YES   NO

3. How satisfied are you with your slide design (the colors and appearance of your slides)?   NOT AT ALL   SOMEWHAT   SATISFIED

4. Have you completed at least two pages of the Who Am I?   YES   NO

5. Have you started to describe a class project?   YES   NO

6. Have you started to digitize a project (through typing, photographs, or scans)?   YES   NO

7. For each subject name the pieces of work that you can put on your portfolio:

    Humanities: 1) _____

    2) _____

    Math: 1) _____

    2) _____

    Science: 1) _____

    2) _____

    Advisory: _____

    Art: _____

    Other: _____

8. Describe what problems or questions you have:

    _____

    _____

    _____

    _____

9. How would you rate your progress overall?   1   2   3   4   5

providing assistance. We also could have done more to recognize the Tech Team members as leaders and tutors, rather than just as the top students who got to get out of class to work on portfolios. Alternatively, we could have used the Tech Team time to provide targeted interventions to help struggling students increase their technological skills, develop deeper understanding of their content work, and accelerate progress on their digital portfolios. Thus, rather than rewarding students who already were achieving success, the students who were initially least engaged in the process would have gained recognition as tech leaders. In fact, by the end of the portfolio process, each student had gained the technical skills necessary to be able to help other students. Even if we weren't able to have a group of peer tutors in the first year, the students would make great tech aides to other students, especially younger ones, in future rollouts of digital portfolios or other PowerPoint work.

Technology proficiency aside, most of my students did not demonstrate the quality and understanding of their portfolio pieces that I expected of them. Much revision of their portfolio pieces was still needed, and many were reluctant to put any effort into revising assignments they had already "completed." Given that the entire purpose of New Day Academy's portfolio assessment was for the students to demonstrate critical thinking, reflective, and revision skills through their best work, gaining these skills was far more important than any aesthetic qualities of their PowerPoint presentations. However, teachers always face the question of how to help their students improve their work and how hard to push them. We want our students to be dedicated and hard-working, their understanding to be developed and accurate, and their final products to be elaborate and presentable. Although a teacher's expectations might occasionally be influenced by whether a student's work will be posted on the classroom or hallway wall or displayed in an exhibition, we primarily want to see the high-level work so we know that students are learning and gaining life values. Still, we cannot expect every student to achieve the same level of work. Each student has a range of learning strengths and struggles and brings a different collection of experiences to the table, so we cannot expect all of them to achieve the same level. The bottom line is that we want to know that

> *The bottom line is that we want to know that our students did their best and that they learned from the process and will be able to show improvement the next time.*

our students did their best and that they learned from the process and will be able to show improvement the next time.

The key is motivating students to want to do their best and to teach them how to get there. Ideally, we are able to help students understand this during the process. I dedicated time to individuals during class, at lunchtime, and after school in the hope that my struggling students would recognize what they were truly capable of. But sometimes they only are able to learn after the fact rather than during the process. I will always remember an experience I had in a writing course my freshman year of college. One Friday morning of finals week, I was still sleeping when the phone rang. (I had just one exam left and was taking advantage of the free time to sleep in.) To my surprise, my writing professor was on the phone. This was the only time I can recall through four years of college that a professor ever called me. He asked me why I hadn't submitted a rewrite of my final paper on the argument for African American reparations. I was fully aware that I had not turned in the rewrite, but I was baffled why the professor would call; after all, I was pretty sure that the rewrite was optional. I fell into a sudden panic that maybe I had misheard, misread, or somehow convinced myself that I didn't *need* to resubmit the paper. When I asked him about it, he responded with an air of surprise: "Well, yeah, it is optional, but don't you *want* to rewrite it?" My answer at that moment was a definite "no," but I would later ask myself if that really had been true. I did want to put forth the best writing piece that I could, didn't I? If I truly wanted to convince a reader about the validity of my argument, I would have to.

I often recall this experience when I find my students putting forth the minimum effort necessary. Why do they act like they just want to "get by" rather than actually succeed? Then I realize that I needed to learn the value of exerting a little extra effort from my own experience. So, although I put in a great deal of extra time to help the students, scaffolded the revision process, previewed the rubric they would be graded on (see Exhibit 5.3) and the questions the evaluators might ask them, and encouraged them to work until they knew they had done their best work, I knew that the students would have to learn from the process and their product on their own. Shawn is one student who appeared to learn from the process. I continuously had to encourage him to add more substance and personality to his digital portfolio. He would make very little progress in class, stating that he would finish it at home or that a piece was already good enough. One day, before I had a chance to discuss with him the many benefits of working from a draft, he returned to school with an empty flash drive, explaining that he was starting over from scratch in order to make a better portfolio presentation.

But when he finished his final portfolio, I knew he still had not put forth his best effort. I think that he knew it as well. Hopefully, he has learned from the experience, as I learned from mine.

For some students, putting too much time into creating an aesthetic presentation was a bigger problem than lack of effort. As the weeks passed, it became evident that the Tech Team and the entire digital portfolio process had been successful in developing the students' technological proficiency. Through their own explorations of PowerPoint's capabilities, as well as individual and class lessons, students discovered a wealth of aesthetic options for how to present their portfolios. Part of this was a valuable learning process, as I wanted to teach them the value of presentation and explained that making a good first impression is essential in the professional and adult world. I explained, for example, that dressing appropriately and professionally for a job interview automatically improves an applicant's chance of being hired; that a university professor (and some high school teachers) might not even read a student's paper if it is hand-written or sloppy; and that some business clients decide whether or not to do business based on the impression they get from the business office. Likewise, their portfolio presentations needed to be visually appealing to their audience. We had some lessons on color management, using the difference between bright yellow text on a neon-green background and dark blue text on a pastel background to explain that good presentation was not just about being pretty or flashy but about being practical. When a student used a photograph or a piece of clip art, I asked how that would help get his or her point across. The lessons were numerous.

For a number of students, the aesthetic choices quickly consumed their work time. It grew into a question of priority: presentation or content. Do you work on making the baking soda and vinegar volcano look good, or do you spend time understanding why a real volcano overflows in the first place? More often than not, the students would choose presentation over working on the content of the portfolio pieces. This was not at all surprising. It was more fun than the portfolio revision process, which many students found to be tedious and hard work. In my experience, many students spent so much time altering the fonts and colors on word processing documents that they hardly gave thought to editing their grammar and spelling. One student in particular became overly caught up in the presentation. Rose battled with a constant feeling that her work was not good enough. PowerPoint software gave her so many options to present her work that she could never find the right way to display a paragraph, word a sentence, color a page, or arrange clip art. She had five versions of the portfolio all saved

Exhibit 5.3. New Day ACADEMY Junior Institute Portfolio Rubric

Junior Institute Portfolio Rubric

Name of Presenter(s): _____

Grader Name: _____

Date: _____

	Perspective	Evidence	Connections	Standards	Presentation
D (4)	- Explains multiple perspectives on the topics. - Assesses strengths and weaknesses of different viewpoints. - Balances positions as a scholar, expert, learner, and student.	- Integrates evidence from various sources, with references. - Provides explanation and proof that is clear, logical, and efficient. - Draws insightful inferences and conclusions from sources. - Independently finds evidence.	- Explicitly connects work artifacts to both subject standards and relevant applications. - Expands on connections between subjects and topics. - Identifies relationships between details and big ideas or themes.	- Displays strong English mechanics and expanded, in-depth writing. - Content knowledge and skills exceed subject area standards.	- Shows superb ownership and pride in presentation. - Clearly and fully introduces, summarizes, and defends pieces. - Presentation shows significant time and effort.
S+(3)	- Shows familiarity with multiple viewpoints. - Presents his/her own opinion on the subjects. - Mostly balances position as a scholar, expert, learner, and student.	- Integrates some evidence sources, with references. - Provides sufficient explanation and proof that can be followed logically. - Draws logical inferences from sources.	- Generally connects work artifacts to subject standards and relevant applications. - Draws connections between subjects and topics. - Differentiates between details and big ideas, causes and effects.	- Displays good English mechanics and expanded writing with only minor errors. - Content knowledge and skills meet the subject area standards.	- Shows ownership and pride in presentation. - Appropriately introduces, summarizes, and defends pieces. - Visual and oral presentations show time and effort.
S(2)	- A few perspectives are considered. - Developed his/her own opinion. - Sometimes balances position as a scholar, expert, learner, and student.	- Contains evidence provided by the teacher. - Provides sufficient explanation and proof to defend arguments. - Shows ability to weigh and interpret evidence.	- Understands relevance of work artifacts and connections to subject content. - Recognizes connections between subjects and topics. - Recognizes causes and effects.	- Generally displays good English mechanics and expanded writing. A few errors might impact readability. - Content knowledge and skills generally meet the subject area standards.	- Shows some ownership and pride in presentation. - Adequately introduces, summarizes, and defends pieces. - Visual and oral presentations are complete.

Differentiated Assessment: How to Assess the Learning Potential of Every Student. Copyright © 2011 by John Wiley & Sons, Inc.

S-(1)	- Begins to identify multiple perspectives. - Begins to form his/her own opinion. - Begins to see differences between position as a scholar, expert, learner, and student.	- Begins to provide evidence, but might interpret incorrectly. - Confuses fact and opinion. - Begins to provide explanation and proof for arguments. - Evidence is inconsistently or not adequately referenced.	- Begins to connect work artifacts to subject content and relevant applications. - Begins to understand connections between subjects. - Confuses details and big picture.	- Displays mostly acceptable English mechanics and writing. - Content knowledge and skills are beginning to meet the subject area standards.	- Begins to show ownership of presentation. - Begins to introduce, summarize, and defend pieces. - Presentation is incomplete but presentable.
NI (0)	- Limited awareness of other viewpoints. - No personal opinion or position. - Takes one position: a scholar, expert, learner, or student.	- Little or no outside evidence. - Provides little or no explanation or proof to defend arguments. - Does not provide references.	- Sees no relevance in the work artifacts. - Recognizes no connections between subjects. - Confuses details and big picture, causes and effects.	- Displays poor English mechanics that make the artifacts difficult to judge. - Content knowledge and skills are far below subject area standards.	- Little or no ownership or pride in presentation. - Lacks introduction, summary, and defense. - Presentation is incomplete.

Total Score: 0 – 4   5 - 8 (no NIs)   9 – 13   14 – 17   18 – 20

(Circle one)   NI   S-   S   S+   D

Your comments:

on her flash disk just in case she decided to go back to a previous version. This caused at least a few moments of panic when she thought that her newest version had been lost, when in reality she had just opened the wrong version. In retrospect, I see it would have been helpful to set a more definitive timeline and to emphasize the breadth of the presentations before encouraging the students to go deep into the details of each page.

I certainly wanted the students' presentations to be beautiful and presentable—and in the end they all were—but I didn't want them to lose sight of the primary goal of portfolios: to demonstrate strong understanding and critical thinking through portfolio pieces. I may have realized this too late for some students. Leslie, for example, who displayed many computer skills but struggled to comprehend texts and grasp big, abstract concepts, constructed a beautiful presentation. Yet when asked to defend her project pieces, she failed to demonstrate a deep knowledge or strong analytical skills for her math project on international currency exchange or for her comparative essay on prejudice during the Civil War and World War II. With a greater focus on her portfolio pieces, she might have been able to demonstrate a stronger understanding. Digital portfolios are but a container—albeit an attractive, effective, and efficient one—through which to exhibit student work. While the digitization of portfolios can improve student understanding and increase reflection, it cannot compensate for the lack of an organized, systematic process of portfolio assessment and reflection or for quality teaching.

In the end, I have no doubt that my advisees' portfolio presentations and their understanding of the work was significantly better than that of students from other classes who did not have the opportunity to create digital portfolios. Digital portfolios helped to further differentiate an assessment process that is already differentiated. Students were able to take advantage of spell check and other assistive technologies, they were given multiple modes of presentation (pictures, sound, video), and the software helped them organize and outline their presentations more effectively. Without the digital portfolio, Leslie may have been even less successful on her portfolio assessment. My students were more engaged in their portfolio work than they had been the previous year, and more than other students. They cooperated with one another, developed valuable technology skills, and took great pride in and ownership of their portfolios. Students were reflecting more on their work, since the process of digitizing it required them to reflect back on their projects or assignments. For the same reason, I would guess that the digital portfolio process improved students' retention of the material they studied.

The biggest complaint students made about the digital portfolios was that they had required too much work, more work than they were used to putting into their portfolios. But that didn't stop them from asking for digital portfolios again the next year. In fact, one student asked me every day—a student teachers still find challenging but who they say has shown tremendous growth. His name is Eric.

TO SUM UP

The case study in this chapter showed how digital portfolios not only served as assessment tools but added to the classroom learning experience. The author describes the process he and his students at New Day Academy went through in a pilot project to create portfolios for year-end assessment.

The student body at the school was approximately half African American and half Hispanic, and most students' scores on state-wide standardized tests were abysmal. School leaders wanted a way to assess student progress that was not based on standardized testing alone and chose digital portfolios. Staff and faculty faced many challenges, including lack of computer equipment, little prior exposure to computers, and finding ways to incorporate portfolio building into the daily classroom routine. Those leading the pilot hoped that their results would motivate the rest of the faculty to participate the following year.

From the students' point of view, being allowed to use computers to display their work was a privilege. Many students created very revealing and thoughtful portfolios, although some were not motivated to do the best possible job or became fixated on the graphics elements over the content.

The author considered the pilot to be a success in that students who had the opportunity to work on digital portfolios had a significantly different learning experience than students in other classes. The team also learned many lessons they could apply when the project was rolled out to the entire school the following year.

- Creating digital portfolios can improve students' motivation and relationships with peers dramatically.

- Standardized tests allow no platform on which to exhibit one's oral and visual skills, whereas portfolios are open-ended.

- Portfolios should be project-based, relevant to the real world, and show problem-solving and critical-thinking skills.

- Portfolios were intended to be more than a collection of students' best work, but also relevant to the real world and demonstrating critical-thinking and problem-solving skills.

- The key is motivating students to do their best and showing them how to do so.

- Because each student brings a range of learning strengths and experiences, we cannot expect them all to achieve at the same level.

- Definitive timelines and an emphasis on content over design details could have helped students better demonstrate the five Habits of Mind in their portfolios.

¿? DISCUSSION QUESTIONS

1. In what ways does a digital portfolio serve as a diagnostic/teaching tool?

2. How can portfolios be used to document students' growth over time?

3. How do they serve as grading/transition tools?

4. What challenges faced the author of this chapter in the start-up phase of the program? As the project progressed?

5. What indirect benefits were gained from students' learning to use computers?

6. What differences did the author point out between the approach elementary students take to their projects and how middle school students handle such assignments? How can middle school students be encouraged?

7. In what ways could the Tech Team have been better used or improved?

8. How did the author keep students on track and monitor their progress? What other ways could have been employed?

9. In what ways could students have been encouraged to do better-quality work? To revise their work when required?

10. What sorts of distractions came up for students? How could these have been handled differently?

NOTE

1. In 2007–2008, New Day Academy's middle school received a C grade from the New York City Department of Education. The high school did not receive a grade because there had not yet been a graduating class, on whose data the high school grade is based.

PART

SEEING STUDENTS' ASSETS: DIFFERENTIATED ASSESSMENT GUIDES INSTRUCTION

CHAPTER

6

DIFFERENTIATED ASSESSMENT, INSTRUCTION, AND ACCOMMODATION

My interest in differentiated assessment and instruction of culturally and linguistically diverse individuals stems from my experience as a multilingual speaker, teacher, and special educator. For nineteen years as a special educator/school psychologist in public and private classrooms in the United States and overseas, I struggled with limitations of standardized testing and assessment strategies used for individuals with diverse language and cultural backgrounds. Tests in English, developed and normed on groups of middle class, native English speakers, were the only tools available to assess and teach multilingual individuals in diverse educational settings. I faced the inherent contradiction of using linguistically and culturally biased assessment tools to evaluate the abilities of individuals, especially adolescents, in their nonnative language. Like many educators, I needed to develop a stronger expertise in using differentiated instruction and authentic assessment to better reflect students' multiple languages, learning styles, and academic abilities, not temporary disabilities in speaking English.

As a special educator and psychologist working in an overseas American school, I recall many individuals whose language and cultural background strongly affected the abilities others could understand. One individual in particular named Arnet was a sixth grader who arrived in my classroom from Israel, dazed and nonverbal. Despite my serious efforts to engage her in classroom activities related to learning English, she remained unresponsive for seven months. She spoke no English or Hebrew at school while sitting day after day in a special setting designed for teaching English language learners from other countries. There were other students who spoke her language in the group but still no response. Hands-on materials, multimedia, direct teaching, games, and other approaches were used by several faculty trained to work with second-language learners. We were completely stumped as she sat and stared at teachers and other students.

Arnet's advocates were her parents, who were fairly fluent in English. They worked for Israeli Airlines and insisted that she was an excellent student in her native language. The school psychologist, speech therapist, counselors, and administrators evaluated her with a collection of instruments, each had his or her favorite tests and she was diagnosed as a possible autistic spectrum case "in serious need of special educational, language development, and psychological services."

The school began to take action to find a placement for her in a class for students with substantial special needs. Arnet had now been sitting in her classes, not speaking, looking glassy-eyed and indicating no comprehension of what teachers or students said to her. The situation appeared grave. It took time to find a space for a thirteen-year-old student, perhaps in another school. In the meantime the evaluation team agreed that she should remain in the class for students with learning and language challenges where ESL instruction took place. One day, as I started to read the fairy tale "Cinderella" to the class, Arnet motioned to me that she wanted the book. I handed it to her, and she stood up in front of the class and articulately read the entire story in English. I was in shock, as we could have labeled her limited in potential as a result of our limited methods of evaluating her abilities.

Despite the rising number of culturally and linguistically diverse students in the United States or in other countries, few educators take time to find the assets in learners who are not learning in typical ways, especially if they speak another language. What can educators do to better understand the language and cultural backgrounds of diverse learners to better assess and teach them?[1]

TABLE 6.1. DIFFERENTIATING INSTRUCTION

Teacher Guidelines	Key Components
Step 1: Know your learners	Ongoing, observation based
	Assessment of students drives instructional planning
Step 2: Design lessons/activities with multiple entry points (posing open-ended questions)	Designing lesson, projects, and assignments that challenge a wide range of learners
Step 3: Pull individuals and small groups to target instruction on a regular basis	Flexible grouping, including whole class, pairs, small groups, and one-on-one tutorials
Step 4: Explain, model, demonstrate, and guide	Balance teaching of key concepts and skills with student-directed learning experiences

How can we define these terms? Table 6.1 outlines the key aspects of considering differentiated instruction as reworking what we teach, how we teach, and the way we teach. To better understand differentiated instruction and assessment for secondary students, I begin by introducing the first step: assessing or knowing your learners through authentic assessment.

Despite the rising number of culturally and linguistically diverse students in the United States or in other countries, few educators take time to find the assets in learners who are not learning in typical ways, especially if they speak another language.

To meet the needs of diverse learners through differentiated instruction, I believe the educational community has to first clarify the distinctions between two misunderstood terms—*evaluation* and *assessment*—which are not equivalent terms. To evaluate is "to ascertain or fix the value or worth of something according to a predetermined set of criteria." On the other hand, "to assess" finds its roots in the Latin *assidere,* which means "to sit beside" to gather information. In this chapter, I define assessment as an interactive process of "sitting beside the learner" to gather authentic and meaningful data to improve student learning, instructional practice, and educational options in the classroom. While evaluation is based only on interpreting students' products, assessment is based on gathering information on the teaching and learning process, the learning products, and the interaction between teacher and learner.

To better understand the nature of educational assessment, as authentic assessment, I believe we should look carefully at the interaction between teacher and learner as they sit beside one another. Whose judgment really counts *in relation to English language learners like Arnet* when it comes to assessing culturally and linguistically diverse adolescents? I believe that classroom teachers' judgments should count, because they are the assessors who know the individuals and observe and sit beside them daily to gather data about their abilities. Perhaps parents' judgments, as in the case of Arnet, should also count in sharing evidence of a learner's previous work in school, bringing samples of student work to help document a student's previous schooling history. "Whose Judgment Counts" are the words of one of the first teachers I studied who identified her expertise in authentic assessment, that is in understanding what multilingual individuals *can* do:

> Whose judgment counts *when it comes to assessing immigrants in our schools? It is usually the school psychologist. Their expertise in assessment—that is,* in giving tests—*is seen as the judgment that counts.*
>
> *If you really want to learn about assessing multilingual individuals, ask the classroom teachers who have years of strategies behind them to use.*
>
> *After about three weeks in my classroom, I can usually tell what an individual needs and how best to teach them, even if they speak little English. (personal interview, 1994)*

KNOWING YOUR LEARNER: UNDERSTAND CULTURAL AND LINGUISTIC ASSETS

An understanding of effective differentiated instructional assessment systems for culturally and linguistically diverse learners is timely and vital to both researchers and practitioners for several reasons. First, changing demographics and the political climate toward multilingual learners in the United States suggests that soon all mainstream educators will be required to know how to effectively assess and teach multilingual populations in their classrooms. Second, early in their educational careers, linguistic minority individuals are often misplaced in special education classrooms, which seriously compromises their opportunity to learn. Current research indicates that teachers often misidentify multilinguals as language or learning disabled, when in reality they are simply limited in English proficiency:

> *Minority over-representation in special education continues as a serious problem.*
>
> *Once a referral is made, the likelihood of testing is high. Once testing takes place, strong gravitational forces toward special education placement are in motion.*
>
> *The referral to assessment to placement rates oscillates between 75 and 90 percent. Once multilingual students are referred for testing, they are placed in special education about 85 percent of the time.*
>
> *Once an individual is placed in special education, despite a mistaken assessment, it takes on average six years to get out. (Fedoruk & Norman, 1990)*

Furthermore, many researchers believe that the misplacement of multilingual learners into special education continues because school leaders and teachers are not knowledgeable about how to assess these individuals (Baca & Almanza, 1991; Hamayan & Damico, 1991), and thus refer them for testing "by experts."

Current research indicates that teachers often misidentify multilinguals as language or learning disabled, when in reality they are simply limited in English proficiency.

This dangerous practice of testing to find a disability must stop, and can only be addressed by better informing practitioners about alternative assessment practices and a different sociocultural framework for the process. By understanding more about the complexities, and the social and cultural aspects of assessment, school leaders and teachers—as the primary agents of change—can stop inappropriate referrals and placements of multilingual students into special education. Simultaneously, both the research and practitioner communities must focus attention on documenting *best practices* in assessment for multilingual students. As Ambert (1991) suggests:

> *The research and practitioner communities are confused about issues of language and culture in relation to learning. Information for researchers, educators, and*

parents is needed on the best assessment and instructional practices for culturally and linguistically diverse individuals . . . practices that give teachers and students actual feedback on teaching and learning. (p. 358)

The process of *assessing culturally and linguistically diverse individuals* is much more complex. It raises important questions about a practitioner's knowledge, skills, and attitudes. First, *the background of the assessor* strongly affects the image of the student that person sees. Does this individual speak another language? Has this person known a nonnative English speaker or lived outside the United States?

Second, *the relationship of the assessor to the learner* affects what that person sees. Is the assessor a psychologist or an educational specialist (trained to study individual behavior) and a stranger to the individual? Is the assessor a classroom teacher (familiar with studying individuals as part of a group) and someone who is familiar with the individual and with his or her capabilities?

Third, *each assessor brings a different lens,* a different kind of expertise to look at the learning. Their expertise determines the:

1. Format—how they approach the assessment process

2. Tools they use—selecting formal tests or informal assessments

3. Time spent—how long they spend with the individual

4. Setting—where they assess the individual (classroom, office, playground)

My practice has taught me that *the context* is a key element in understanding what any individual knows, especially a multilingual individual. The closer and more frequently assessors look, the clearer they can see the language and learning abilities of an individual. A classroom teacher collects many "episodes of learning" (Wolf, 1989) in daily observations, providing a much fuller picture of the individual's strengths and weaknesses.

KNOWING YOUR LEARNERS: BUILDING A COMPREHENSIVE ASSESSMENT SYSTEM

Reflecting a sociocultural approach, Alvarez (1991) refers to these classroom approaches as "assessment embedded in instruction" (p. 284), which is defined as a set of assessment strategies for all individuals. These strategies are directly linked to daily instruction and focus on the setting (ecological assessment); the pedagogy (curriculum-based assessment); and the process of teacher-student interaction (portfolio assessment).[2]

CLASSROOM ASSESSMENT RESEARCH SUGGESTIONS

Consider curriculum-based assessments to:

1. Observe the student, the classroom environment, teaching format, and peer interactions

2. Document and keep track of achievement levels in content areas using classroom materials using student work

3. Observe student responses to what is known, what needs to be taught, and the pace of instruction

4. Keep track of student performance using samples of student work and portfolios

Overall, a body of the recent research points to a changing picture of assessment for multilingual individuals. In the United States, the literature suggests a move away from formal toward informal assessment (Genesee & Hamayan, 1994; Gonzalez, 1998; Harris Stefanakis, 2002; Hernandez, 1994; Wiggins, 1989; Wolf, 1989). The trend is to create assessment tools that more accurately reflect learning *in context*, and to gather information from specialists, teachers, and family members (Baca & Clark, 1992; Damico et al., 1992; DeLeon, 1990; Dolson, 1994; Gonzalez, 1998; Harris Stefanakis, 1998; Wilkinson, 1992). Whether labeled "authentic" or "alternative assessment," the goal is to gather information *from a variety of sources* while *sitting beside the learner*.

Overall, I recommend, based on recent research, using a *wider lens* for looking at assessment practice with multilingual individuals. This means creating a comprehensive assessment system to *combine formal and informal* assessments to assess language proficiency and cognitive abilities both in test situations and in the context of daily learning situations. Therefore, *observations, interviews, and portfolios of student work* are informal assessment materials that should be added to information from standardized test results. Further, I recommend combining formal, informal, and classroom assessment to balance the needs of system-level compliance (formal) with "individual-centered assessment" (informal/classroom) (Dolson, 1994; Genishi, 1992).

USING THE STUDENT'S ASSETS: SOCIOCULTURAL FRAMEWORK TO DIFFERENTIATE ASSESSMENT

A sociocultural perspective assumes that individuals learn language in real-life situations that depend on social interactions and that multilingual individuals display a different knowledge and use of language depending on the social context. The sociocultural perspective makes three assumptions:

1. Multilingualism is a potential cognitive asset that can enhance learning (Hakuta & Garcia, 1989).

2. Sociocultural factors affect learning, and context is the key to understanding language output (Cummins, 1986, 1989; Snow, 1992).

3. Language proficiency and related learning abilities should be assessed in context and over time (Baca & Almanza, 1991; Damico, 1991; DeLeon, 1990; Dolson, 1994).

My research suggests that a stronger definition for differentiated assessment is needed:

Differentiated assessment . . . is a process that facilitates appropriate instructional decisions by providing information on two fundamental questions:

1. How are we (teacher and learner) doing?
2. How can we do better?

These two questions assume that the teacher *and* learner are equally vital in assessing the learning process. This means that classroom assessment becomes an interactive process whereby teachers "sit beside" individuals to assess and to teach them. If this idea holds, then classroom assessment becomes a model that realigns the power relationship between the potentially dominant teacher and dominated individual. If the interaction between teacher and learner equalizes the power relationships, then *both what teachers do and what students do* during learning activities must be looked at, simultaneously and not in isolation. Studying differentiated assessment of skilled teachers' individual practices, their process for knowing their learners and gathering information, which includes observing, recording, questioning, interviewing, and collecting student work, are strikingly similar.

To capture what experienced teachers say, they suggest that classroom assessment is a process, but it does have patterns they follow that they suggest allow them to actively link assessment and instruction of diverse individuals as well as small groups.

BASIC PREMISES: DIFFERENTIATED ASSESSMENT

1. A classroom has a culture, and other individuals, acting as cultural brokers, can communicate that culture to help a new multilingual individual adjust.

2. Understanding the differences between a multilingual individual's home culture and school culture is vital to any assessment process, which begins with ongoing dialogue between parents and teachers.

3. Individuals may have more, not less, going on cognitively, yet accessing what they know may take time, interpretation, and translation on the part of teachers and parents.

These teachers also recognized that each student's learning process involves complex issues of language and culture, which require a more extensive classroom assessment process. Best-practice teachers follow a sociocultural framework for assessment that looks first at social interactions, then at issues of culture and language, and then learning skills.

CLASSROOM PERFORMANCE ASSESSMENTS

Differentiating assessment documents the process and products of student learning and helps teachers understand what a learner knows and can do. What is differentiated assessment (DA) linked to instruction (DI) using a sociocultural approach? Carol Tomlinson and her colleagues (1995), the originators of DI, offer a collection of writings to define differentiated instruction. Adapting these ideas to culturally and linguistically exceptional learners, I summarize elements of differentiating instruction in the feature "How to Assess Learning Abilities."

DIFFERENTIATED INSTRUCTION: KNOWING YOUR LEARNERS AND FINDING THEIR STRENGTHS

If the assessment of diverse students is to drive instructional practice, then ongoing observation of learners and their learning is the first step to differentiated instruction. Multiple intelligences theory (Gardner, 1983) provides a framework

HOW TO ASSESS LEARNING ABILITIES

Differentiating instruction strategies include:

- Multiple entry points—Designing activities that are open-ended, at different levels (tiered assignments)

- Anchor activities—Familiar self-sustaining activity so teacher can rotate and work with groups

- Flexible grouping—Assigning students to groups based on readiness, learning styles, and interests—working with two, then three or four people

for profiling the learning abilities of individuals in an educational setting, especially those with cultural and linguistic diversity. In the graphic representing Gardner's eight intelligences (see Figure 6.1), I present a way to remember each intelligence with an icon and to link prior knowledge with new knowledge. On the left side are "the intelligences," according to Gardner's theory (1983,

Figure 6.1.   Multiple Intelligences Checklist

KNOW YOUR LEARNER MATERIALS IN MI/PORTFOLIOS

The Eight Intelligences (Gardner, 1997)

Linguistic Intelligence		Bodily Kinesthetic Intelligence	
Mathematical Intelligence		Visual Spatial Intelligence	
Interpersonal Intelligence		Musical Intelligence	
Intrapersonal Intelligence		Naturalistic Intelligence	

Source: Harris Stefanakis, 2003.

DIFFERENTIATED INSTRUCTION—STEP BY STEP

Step 1: Differentiate—KNOW YOUR LEARNER

DI CAS (Comprehensive Assessment System)

Find their assets: Multiple intelligences

Step 2: Differentiated Instruction

Common planning format—INQUIRY (Norms)

Lesson study—Lesson design tools

Consider assistive technology (tools)

1993, 1997) often used by our educational community in classrooms (linguistic, mathematical, interpersonal, and intrapersonal).

On the right side are the intelligences that need further recognition and attention by leaders and teachers in their work with students (bodily kinesthetic, visual spatial, musical, and naturalistic). Learning more through observing, keeping track and documenting a student's learning with attention focused on the intelligences may help teachers discover a student's assets, often not readily visible in daily classroom activities.

Multiple intelligences theory provides a framework for profiling the learning abilities of individuals in an educational setting, especially those with cultural and linguistic diversity.

Using MI theory as a way to observe the process and products of student learning can help teachers obtain a fuller picture of a student's abilities. Student self-assessment, more often easily understood in terms of learning styles, can offer a profile of strengths so teachers know their learners and can begin planning to differentiate their instruction, as shown in Figure 6.2. How does a classroom teacher with twenty to thirty students do this, given the learning challenges presented?

Figure 6.2. Building a Profile of a Learner

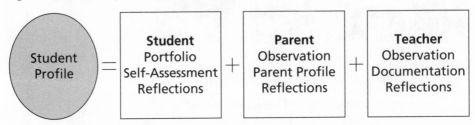

CREATING A STUDENT PROFILE: A TEACHER'S STORY OF DIFFERENTIATED INSTRUCTION

To understand the diversity of individuals and to build a learning profile, Kathleen, a teacher in an inclusion class, practices researching each individual by assessing and *sitting beside a learner* (Harris Stefanakis, 1998a). Through systematically looking at each individual's daily work, a teacher can learn more about the individual and what he or she really knows and can do. By observing and recording, along with collecting and reflecting on student work, Kathleen creates *a profile* of the multiple intelligences of individual students in her group of third graders. Her classroom of twenty-four students in a Cambridge, Massachusetts, school has four or five who are exceptional learners and two others who have disabilities.

To create a student's profile using MI theory, Kathleen considers what she observes about each individual using the lens of linguistic, logical-mathematical, musical-rhythmic, interpersonal, intrapersonal, visual-spatial, bodily-kinesthetic, and naturalistic intelligences (Gardner 1983, 1993, 1997). Through daily classroom interactions, discussions, and observations of what individuals do and make as work samples, she informally assesses each individual's skills and abilities while she teaches the class. In her description, she uses her "profile" of Fallon, a challenging student, to distinguish a learning problem from a language acquisition issue:

> *The individual who comes to mind is Fallon, because she had auditory processing issues. She had been tested over and over and I read the report and put it over there. It did not teach me what she could do [how she was smart]. I needed to know what she can do and where to begin to best teach her since reading was a serious challenge.*
>
> *I find out so much more by being with the individual and looking at student work than from test reports . . . on paper. From watching her over time, I learned*

that she has difficulty with language that goes beyond being multilingual and beyond any developmental questions. I know there are strengths and there has been progress with her, but it has been slow.

Kathleen assumes she will find a way to determine "how Fallon is smart" even though others' observations may not indicate this. She begins by assessing—*sitting beside the learner*—to discover what she *can* do, and uses MI to systematically look at what this individual does well and where she struggles. Kathleen describes her observations of Fallon's classroom interactions and keeps track of her work samples while teaching:

Sometimes I get really frustrated because progress is slow. I start collecting all these little pieces of work weekly that show me that she is making progress. She is developing in areas of literacy in the words she prints and recalls, and I have confidence that reading complex text and understanding it will happen.

I see her as a capable artist, as a scientist, as a cooperative learner, a musician. She may not be reading and understanding fluently and easily, but she is capable in many other ways.

I thought that she was only speaking Portuguese at home. I was confused, since she speaks mostly Portuguese with her mother, and her father speaks English. I learned that he is not home that much, so she is basically using Portuguese. I tried strategies for reading—oral, visual-spatial, kinesthetic, lyrical—and I found that she really had some visual strengths . . . visual memory is one. I could see what she can do by collecting information—little assessments. To teach a challenging individual like her, this is what works.

I learned by sitting beside her she is still confusing the two languages, although she cannot remember the names of the letters. While teaching her, I found that if I give a sound to her, she can identify the letter. If she hears a rhythm, she can blend a letter. Yes, she is making progress because we were able to try different strategies.

Kathleen created an MI profile to guide her future programming for Fallon:

I see she knows where to look in the classroom to get help to use the visual cues in the environment . . . she copies from a chart or anywhere she can see a word. She is really capable of learning cognitively.

I see a lot going on. I never really thought too much about individual issues until I came to this class, and in here we have such a variety of learners who may not seem capable but they are.

For Kathleen, MI becomes an analytic tool for her ongoing observation of Fallon. By sitting beside Fallon, and creating a profile of her strengths in different learning situations, she has found a window into this individual's learning.

DIFFERENTIATED INSTRUCTION: KNOWING INDIVIDUAL LEARNERS' MULTIPLE INTELLIGENCES

Applying the theory of multiple intelligences means first understanding that all individuals have at least eight intelligences, many of which do not show up in traditional classroom activities (which focus on linguistic and mathematical intelligences). This suggests that teachers shift from a notion of measuring intelligence and student learning to a new notion of understanding students' multiple intelligences by observing and documenting a collection of their work to create a profile of abilities.

All individuals have at least eight intelligences, many of which do not show up in traditional classroom activities (which focus on linguistic and mathematical intelligences).

Second, to better understand each individual's unique profile of intelligences requires a shift in the position of power between teacher and learner. Teachers have to redesign learning tasks, more often sitting beside individual learners to see *how they best learn* and to *listen to* what they say about their own learning. Knowing them better means teaching them better. This personalization creates a more inclusive learning environment for the individual student, as well as the collection of students in the class. The examples are tools to assist readers in doing profiles of their students.

TO SUM UP

The author explains the process she went through to develop more differentiated instruction and assessment that reflected students' multiple learning styles and academic abilities rather than deficient English skills. She gives examples of ways in which teachers can assess learning through sitting with students and describes what some other teachers have done to use differentiated assessment.

A sociocultural approach to assessment means observing each student in the classroom environment, documenting and tracking achievement levels, and using samples of his or her work from different points in time.

KEY POINTS: APPLYING MULTIPLE INTELLIGENCES

- All learners have all eight intelligences. They are channels for learning, not ways to label student abilities.

- Individuals have unique profiles based on all of the multiple intelligences; areas of strength can become ways to address areas of weakness. *(bridging)*

- Multiple intelligences theory is an analytical tool to help educators assess and teach all students—to reach more individuals.

For additional resources on multiple intelligences, please see the DVD for this book.

Understanding the differences between a multilingual individual's home culture and school culture is vital to any assessment process, which begins with dialogue between parents and teachers. Individuals may have more, not less, going on cognitively, yet accessing what they know may take time, multiple interpretation, and translation on the part of teachers and parents.

Multiple intelligence models provide a way for educators to look at students in a broader way.

- The educational community must understand the distinctions between evaluation and assessment.

- Assessment can be defined as the interactive process of *sitting beside* students in order to gather information.

- Classroom teachers' judgment should count because they know their students' capacities best. Parents also can offer insight into the situation.

- The background of the assessor and his or her relationship with the learner influence what he or she sees.

- Differentiated assessment documents the process and products of student learning and helps teachers understand what the learner knows and can do.

- Student self-assessments can be used to determine students' learning style and strengths.

¿? DISCUSSION QUESTIONS

1. What can educators do to better understand the language and cultural backgrounds of diverse students in order to assess and teach them?

2. In what ways can teachers "sit beside" their students? What can they learn from the experience?

3. Why is it particularly important to move to differentiated instructional assessment now?

4. If standardized tests look for student deficiencies, what differentiated assessments should be used to judge?

5. Would you add or subtract anything to the definition of differentiated assessment given in the chapter? If so, what? Why?

6. How could you design instruction with multiple entry points and flexible grouping in order to differentiate among students' abilities?

7. How can the assessment of diverse students drive better instructional practice?

8. Discuss ways each of the eight intelligences can be "tested" in the classroom and through assignments.

9. In what ways can student self-assessments be incorporated into the curriculum?

10. How can a classroom teacher find time and ways to differentiate instruction? Assessment? List some specific methods.

NOTES

1. This chapter offers research-based solutions to the complex challenge of assessing the strengths of multilingual learners. Briefly I summarize what I have learned about the assessment of multilingual individuals, based on twenty years of classroom teaching and nine years of research, as chronicled in my book *Whose Judgment Counts?* (1998b).

2. For a more complete review of the classroom assessment literature, see pages 15 through 18 of my book *Whose Judgment Counts?* (1998b).

CHAPTER

7

HOW DIFFERENTIATED ASSESSMENT GUIDES INSTRUCTION

Voices from the Field

To provide a case study of differentiated assessment in action in a classroom, I offer the story of Miguel Guitierrez, a twenty-year veteran of the Cambridge Public Schools trained in both elementary and secondary programs. Miguel describes using differentiated assessment as a learning experience, one that helped him to define his instructional practice and to differentiate his teaching. Student portfolios, he suggests, help him understand the complexity of individual learners' academic, social, cultural, and linguistic backgrounds. They also guide his development of activities at different levels and with multiple entry points in order to accommodate his students' diverse skills and abilities. He uses anchor activities, such as journaling, charting, or graphing, to keep the whole group engaged while he rotates among learners who may need more direct instruction or more independence. Miguel thus practices the art of flexible grouping, thinking about students' readiness, learning styles, or interests, depending on the subject he is teaching. Here I describe how this works in practice.

STRATEGIES DIFFERENTIATING INSTRUCTION (DESIGNING COLLABORATIVE GROUPS)

Content: Examine the Curriculum—Decide What to Teach

- Choose key concepts and topics essential to deeper understanding.
- Develop tiered assignments (see the planning tool in Figure 7.6).

Process: Decide What and How to Teach Key Ideas

- Combine anchor and teacher-directed activities.
- Begin adding group work with pairs, trios, and then groups of four.
- Assign roles of time keeper, facilitator, record keeper, and spokesperson, and rotate these in each group.

Products: Decide on Multiple Formats for Assessment/Use Rubrics

- Assess before and after instruction.
- Gather data in writing and graphically using graphic organizers.

KNOWING YOUR LEARNERS: USING PORTFOLIOS TO DIFFERENTIATE ASSESSMENT

In the urban public school where he works, Miguel keeps track of students' progress by collecting work samples in portfolios created for each individual in his class. These portfolios are collections of work that students select to show their growth in literacy and other subject areas. Miguel and his students define portfolios as a place to keep student work. They provide evidence of what each individual cares about and learns. As Miguel explains:

> I keep a portfolio of the individuals' projects, drafts, writing, and other things they make in a folder. This to me is the data on an individual. I look at the piece of work when the individual is making it.
>
> I listen to what the individuals say about this work. I try to make a note on the back of the paper of what they are telling me. I ask them if they think this piece of work is something they want to save for their portfolios.

We decide together which pieces to save for their parent conferences or for their final grading and reflection. Usually they surprise me and choose memorable pieces that show lots of growth.

Miguel's students keep this work—essentially the data on their learning—in their individual folders. Students then periodically select and reflect on their work as evidence of growth in a certain area. Working on the collection, selection, and reflection of portfolio items is a part of the weekly routine.

So how does the process work? Miguel sets aside 35 minutes, or one period a week, after lunch on Fridays as his class's portfolio assessment and reflection time. Each student looks back through his or her weekly collection of work, making sure each piece is dated. They select two or three pieces that show growth for that week and write reflections on these pieces. These weekly selections and the corresponding reflections are stapled, tagged, and saved in another folder as portfolio entries. While students are writing reflections, Miguel meets with a few of them to discuss their work. He keeps a calendar at his desk so students can sign up for their monthly portfolio conferences.

Students know the date on which they will share their work with Miguel and may rehearse describing what they are doing. Miguel has a system built into his daily routine to sit beside as many students as possible each day. This is how he and the other teachers make portfolios a part of their daily routine.

The three key steps in the portfolio process are collecting work, selecting items that demonstrate growth, and reflecting on what the selected pieces demonstrate about the students and their learning. This is illustrated in Figure 7.1

Figure 7.1. The Process of Building Portfolios into Classrooms

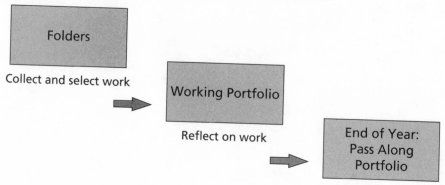

Folders

Collect and select work

Working Portfolio

Reflect on work

End of Year: Pass Along Portfolio

To teach students how to reflect on their work, Miguel uses three key questions. He repeats these questions orally and in writing:

1. What did you do in this piece of work? (Describe the assignment and your response.)

2. How did you do it? (Describe your process, including materials used.)

3. What did you learn from this piece of work? What surprised you about this work?

Miguel admits:

Yes, some families talk to their [child] and reflect on what they do, but I find that most individuals need to be taught how to reflect on what they do. In my experience, individuals need to be given new language for how to express their reflections in writing beyond "I like it, it's my best, it looks good." Details of the work and its creation are what we need to learn how to describe and write about.

We practice writing reflections during group meeting time and I create a chart of key vocabulary (words and phrases) to help them say (1) what they did and (2) how they did it.

To facilitate the collection, selection, and reflection process, Miguel prepares weekly reflection sheets (see Exhibit 7.1) that are attached to pieces selected for the portfolio. Students look back at the pieces they select and fill in their responses to the key questions.

Exhibit 7.1. Sample Reflection Sheets

Ages 13–15
Caring for SELF, FRIENDS & FAMILY

How? When? Where? does s/he do these things now? Feel free to check, underline, make notes everywhere!

BEING A FRIEND

1. Initiating and maintaining relationships
   - meeting and making friends
   - helping friends with projects/chores
   - helping friends learn new things
   - helping friends solve problems
   - having a pen pal
   - including a variety of friends in activities
2. Communicating with friends
   - phoning friends
   - writing letters
   - e-mailing friends
3. Social activities
   - planning events/activities
   - having/going to parties
   - spending time with friends
   - having/attending sleepovers
   - participating in team/group activities

FAMILY MEMBERSHIP

4. Family fun
   - participating in celebrations
   - visiting relatives
   - participating in vacations and holidays
5. Kitchen
   - helping cook
   - making meals/following recipes
   - setting/clearing table
   - washing/drying dishes
   - using dishwasher
   - putting dishes away
   - helping with grocery shopping
   - putting food/groceries away
   - sorting recyclables
   - taking out the trash
6. Bedroom
   - making bed
   - picking up/putting away belongings
   - cleaning room
7. Outside
   - yard work
   - bringing in firewood
   - washing car
   - maintaining bike
   - working on car/motorcycle
8. Miscellaneous chores
   - sibling care
   - pet care
   - getting mail
   - running errands
   - doing laundry
   - dusting/sweeping/vacuuming
   - helping with household projects: painting, washing windows

Which ones does s/he want to do more?

Which ones does s/he want to do more?

Activity-Based Assessment
Inventory

If students are struggling to write, Miguel has them record their reflections, or he asks a student volunteer to help record what their classmates say on the reflection sheet. This simple modification of the reflection process is particularly useful for individuals who are English language learners or have special needs that make written expression a challenge.

The student portfolio is one part of the documentation about his students' progress that Miguel uses at meetings with parents and other teachers. His recorded observations of individuals and notes on their daily activities add to this assessment collection and help him compile a profile of his students' multiple intelligences (MI) (Gardner, 1983), as shown in Figure 7.2.

At the end of the year, Miguel's students compile ten to twelve work samples they have selected and reflected on, which represent their progress throughout the school year. This collection is called the pass-along portfolio.

MULTIPLE ENTRY POINTS TO INSTRUCTION: THE PHYSICAL ENVIRONMENT SUPPORTS LEARNING

The organization of Miguel's classroom space reflects his philosophy of teaching and learning as a sociocultural process based on interaction. Because his goal is to create a community of learners, he believes that the classroom spaces should allow for work in small groups, where individual possessions and boundaries do not curtail student interaction. As Miguel explains, "I want to create a community in this room and a sense that the work we do is done together. I am trying to design this into the physical space in this classroom."

> *"I want to create a community in this room and a sense that the work we do is done together. I am trying to design this into the physical space in this classroom."*

My observations in his classroom suggest that the physical environment helps create a setting in which Miguel can observe and interact frequently with each student, which allows him to compile a profile of each one's learning. Individual and group work take place in small, separate areas. Chairs are strategically placed where Miguel can observe one individual closely and keep track of six others (see Figure 7.3). Both he and his assistant are strategic observers and informal assessors of individual students as an integral part of their daily teaching.

Figure 7.2. Learning Profile

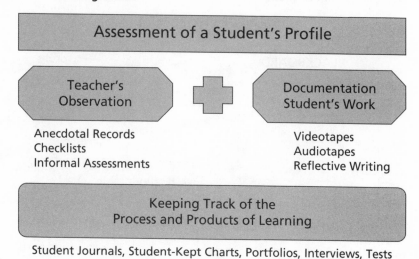

Assessment of a Student's Profile

Teacher's Observation

Documentation Student's Work

Anecdotal Records
Checklists
Informal Assessments

Videotapes
Audiotapes
Reflective Writing

Keeping Track of the
Process and Products of Learning

Student Journals, Student-Kept Charts, Portfolios, Interviews, Tests

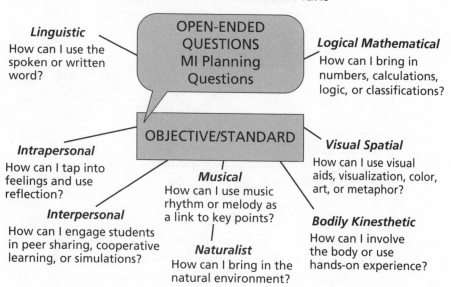

MI Organization Framework for Thematic Units or Lesson Plans

OPEN-ENDED QUESTIONS MI Planning Questions

OBJECTIVE/STANDARD

Linguistic
How can I use the spoken or written word?

Logical Mathematical
How can I bring in numbers, calculations, logic, or classifications?

Intrapersonal
How can I tap into feelings and use reflection?

Visual Spatial
How can I use visual aids, visualization, color, art, or metaphor?

Musical
How can I use music rhythm or melody as a link to key points?

Interpersonal
How can I engage students in peer sharing, cooperative learning, or simulations?

Bodily Kinesthetic
How can I involve the body or use hands-on experience?

Naturalist
How can I bring in the natural environment?

Figure 7.3.   Classroom Diagram

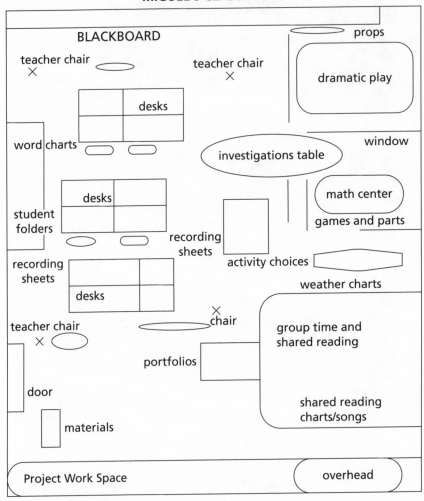

MIGUEL'S CLASSROOM

X = Teacher observation spot

To foster group interaction and improve the chances of reaching every individual using multiple intelligences theory, Miguel thinks carefully about his plans for the physical space. He creates centers that display materials for students to use, which combine at least two or three intelligences and offer activities with multiple means of expression—words, pictures, art, graphics, charts, and audiotapes. Miguel uses a checklist (Figure 7.4) to track his use of the multiple intelligences, which serves as a reflective tool.

Figure 7.4. Multiple Intelligences Checklist

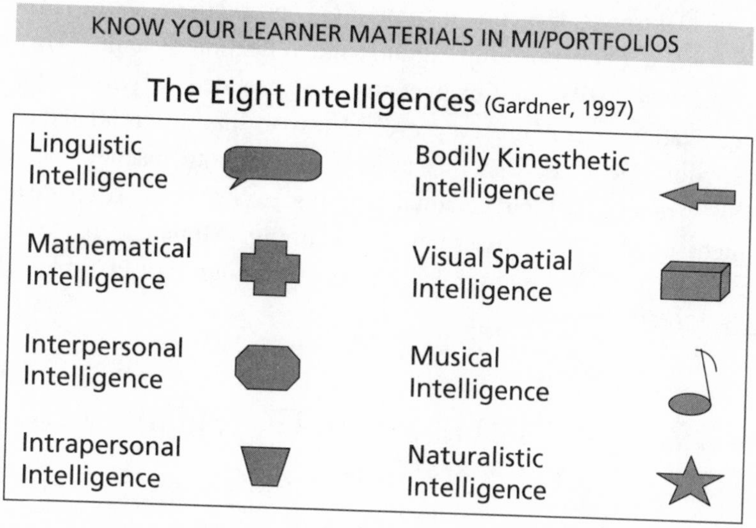

KNOW YOUR LEARNER MATERIALS IN MI/PORTFOLIOS

The Eight Intelligences (Gardner, 1997)

Linguistic Intelligence		Bodily Kinesthetic Intelligence	
Mathematical Intelligence		Visual Spatial Intelligence	
Interpersonal Intelligence		Musical Intelligence	
Intrapersonal Intelligence		Naturalistic Intelligence	

Source: Harris Stefanakis, 2003.

Miguel's classroom is designed so that he can actively assess his students by sitting beside them. He uses his classroom assessments to offer his students personalized opportunities for differentiated learning, including MI-based activities. He finds that creating focused activities that draw on linguistic or logical mathematical intelligence is fairly simple, but areas for music, art, and exploration of nature need to be worked on systematically. In his classroom design, Miguel works to include all the intelligences that are often represented more concretely in specific activity areas:

- Linguistic/interpersonal—demonstrated in group meeting, library, reading area

- Logical mathematical/interpersonal—demonstrated in games, math manipulatives

- Musical—demonstrated in group meeting, computer, DVD area, and slogans posted

- Visual spatial/kinesthetic/interpersonal—demonstrated in art center, chart area

- Naturalist/interpersonal/kinesthetic—demonstrated in group meeting, science center

Miguel continuously observes individuals and small groups and their preferences in the classroom. The combination of (1) observational tools, (2) collections of student work, (3) a portfolio-tagging and reflection system, (4) rubrics for assignments, and (5) the optional center for extended activities in the classroom organization offer Miguel a powerful way to link differentiated assessment and instruction. He notes that this system invites both teacher and learner to continuously reflect on their personal learning experiences. After designing an environment conducive to assessing for learning, Miguel turns to his lesson designs, where he uses the multiple entry points design tool in Table 7.1 (Harris Stefanakis, 2003).

TABLE 7.1. ADDITIONAL STRATEGIES FOR DIFFERENTIATING INSTRUCTION

Formats	Strategies
Stations—different areas, different activities	**Entry points**—explore topic via
	1. Narration—Story
	2. Logical quantitative—numbers, deductive reasoning
	3. Foundational—examining philosophy/vocabulary
	4. Aesthetic—sensory, hands-on
Compacting—assess students before units, students who know content work on alternative learning packets	
Agendas—personalized lists of tasks in a given time	

ANCHOR ACTIVITIES AND FLEXIBLE GROUPING

Each day, Miguel roams around the classroom, checking in on each individual's reading and journal writing. His morning schedule begins with 15 minutes of journal writing, a "Do-Now" activity, and drawing. After journal time, students write answers to open-ended questions related to problem solving. Miguel designs his daily assignments by drawing from ideas expressed in student journals. These classroom conversations, which are built into independent writing time, allow Miguel "to size up," in Airasian's (1990) words, each individual's personal thoughts and daily written work. When he stops to look at a student's work, he questions that student about the piece he or she is working on, asking why he or she does it that way.

These student-teacher interactions allow time for personalized or differentiated teaching when, as Miguel suggests, he identifies areas to edit and teaches them how to improve their writing. In essence, he is scaffolding the individual's learning process by continuously asking questions, asking for revisions, and observing his or her responses:

> As I watch six individuals doing journals, I see they are confused about the words there, their, and they're. I stopped the whole group. I asked them to tell me when each of these words is used and I quickly do a mini-lesson on the board so I am responding to this teachable moment.
>
> They edit their journals and promise me that they understand this now. They know I look to see how to use and spell these words. I ask them in their work to show me they understand specific spellings, meanings, and usage.

DIFFERENTIATING INSTRUCTION: LESSON AND UNIT DEVELOPMENT FOR SECONDARY STUDENTS

How do elementary, middle school, and high school teachers develop lessons and units to accommodate culturally and linguistically exceptional learners, given the focus on content and the pressures of high-stakes tests? The challenge for all teachers who work with diverse learners is to create lessons that offer multiple entry points, tiered assignments, and flexible grouping using national and/or state curricular frameworks that mandate what students must know and be able to do. A pyramid planning tool, shown in Figure 7.5, offers a framework for thinking and planning in order to differentiate instruction and assessment for units or lessons.

VOICES FROM THE FIELD: DIFFERENTIATED INSTRUCTION AT THE HIGH SCHOOL LEVEL

As a team of instructors for grade 9, Jed, Jenna, and Dorothy developed the following lesson in the figure to differentiate instruction for their mixed-ability English class. They began by profiling their learners and then considering (1) what all students must learn, based on curriculum mandates and test requirements; (2) what most students will learn; and (3) what some students will learn. Their differentiated lesson plan was shared with the entire class, using the framework and materials shown in Figure 7.5.

DIFFERENTIATED CURRICULUM: MEETING THE NEEDS OF ALL LEARNERS

The unit-planning pyramid is a process teachers use to plan the content for their students in subject-area classes. It entails considering the content to be taught by using a mental template of a graphic device called the planning pyramid (see Figure 7.6), self-questioning techniques, and completion of the unit planning form. This process is used to focus attention on what content will be learned by all students, what content will be learned by some students, and how that learning will be directed.

What Results Can Be Expected?

Use of the planning pyramid enables teachers to become more explicit about what they want students to learn and more proficient in planning units to promote the learning for all students.

How Is It Used?

Use of the planning pyramid enables teachers to become more explicit about what they want students to learn and more proficient in planning units to promote the learning for all students.

The method that employs the unit planning form involves the use of a graphic device designed to guide teachers' thinking and help them meet the challenge of planning content in general education classes that include individuals with a broad range of needs. The pyramid is a way of considering what needs to be taught so that all students have the opportunity to learn.

Figure 7.5. Differentiated Lesson/Unit with Tiered Assignments

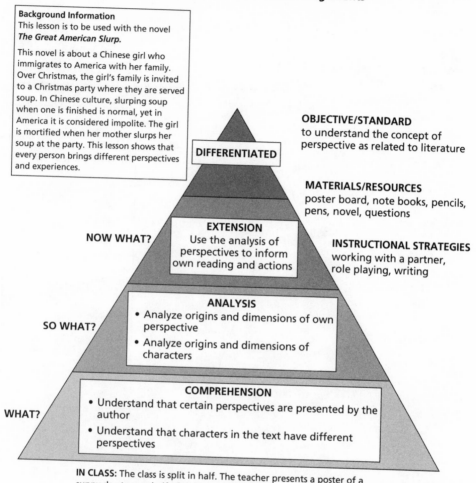

Background Information
This lesson is to be used with the novel *The Great American Slurp*.

This novel is about a Chinese girl who immigrates to America with her family. Over Christmas, the girl's family is invited to a Christmas party where they are served soup. In Chinese culture, slurping soup when one is finished is normal, yet in America it is considered impolite. The girl is mortified when her mother slurps her soup at the party. This lesson shows that every person brings different perspectives and experiences.

DIFFERENTIATED

OBJECTIVE/STANDARD
to understand the concept of perspective as related to literature

MATERIALS/RESOURCES
poster board, note books, pencils, pens, novel, questions

NOW WHAT?

EXTENSION
Use the analysis of perspectives to inform own reading and actions

INSTRUCTIONAL STRATEGIES
working with a partner, role playing, writing

SO WHAT?

ANALYSIS
• Analyze origins and dimensions of own perspective
• Analyze origins and dimensions of characters

WHAT?

COMPREHENSION
• Understand that certain perspectives are presented by the author
• Understand that characters in the text have different perspectives

IN CLASS: The class is split in half. The teacher presents a poster of a sunny day to one-half of the class and one of a wintry day to the other half. Students write about what they would do on this kind of day. They are paired with students who see the other poster and discuss their different perspectives. The class then discusses how this relates to the novel and role plays scenes from the novel.

HOMEWORK: Students choose a character from the text and write a journal entry from that character's perspective.

The lesson planning pyramid is divided into three levels of learning (see Figure 7.6):

■ The base or largest section of the pyramid represents the most important concepts in a unit that teachers want their students to master. Information at

Figure 7.6. Planning Pyramid

Lesson Planning Form, Date: _____

Unit:
Instructional Strategies/Adaptations:
In-class Assignments:

Lesson Objectives:

Material/Resources:

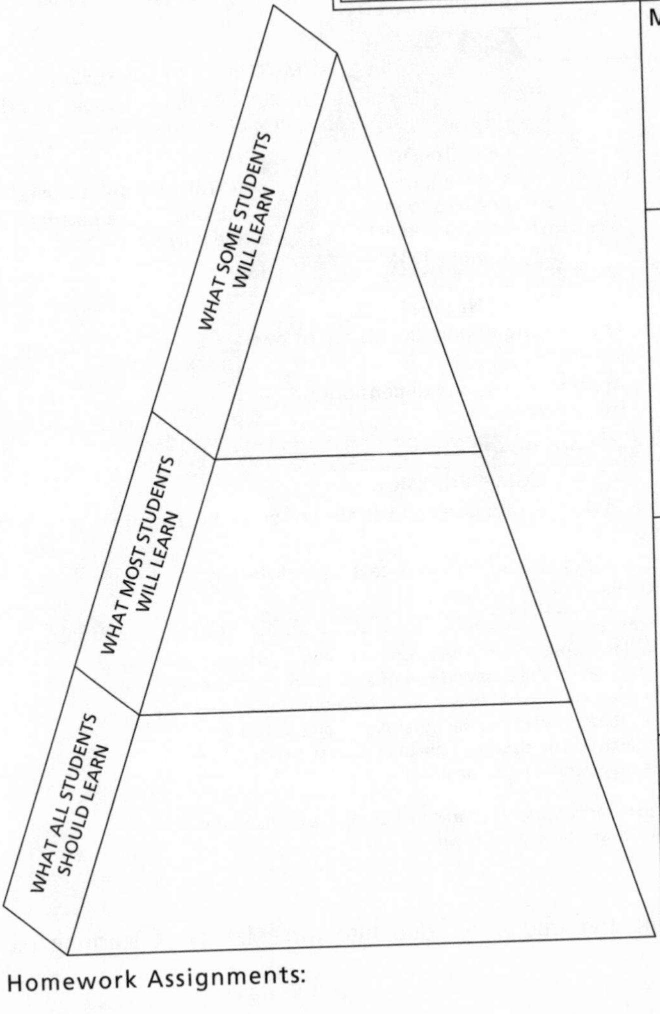

WHAT SOME STUDENTS WILL LEARN

WHAT MOST STUDENTS WILL LEARN

WHAT ALL STUDENTS SHOULD LEARN

Homework Assignments:

this level may be conceptualized more broadly and generally than at succeeding levels. The guiding question that teachers must ask themselves relative to the pyramid base is, "What do I want ALL students to learn?"

- The next level of the pyramid represents the level of information the teachers consider to be next in importance for understanding the content/concepts of the unit. It can include additional facts, extensions of base concepts, related concepts, and/or more complex concepts. The guiding question associated with this level is, "What do I want MOST students to learn?"

- The top level of the pyramid represents information the teacher considers supplementary. This information is more complex or detailed and will be mastered by the fewest students in the classroom. The guiding question here is, "What information may SOME students learn?"

The lesson-planning pyramid enables teachers to become more explicit about what they want students to learn. Teachers take time to answer questions for themselves:

- What learning strategies do my students know, or need to learn, to master these concepts?

- What in-class and homework assignments are appropriate for this lesson?

- Do some assignments need to be adapted for individuals with special needs?

- How will I monitor student learning on an ongoing, informal basis?

- How will I assess student learning at the end of the lesson?

- How will I assess student learning of lesson material at the end of the unit?

Using the planning pyramid, teachers generate specific ideas that allow them to:

1. Structure an agenda for the lesson
2. List materials to be gathered and used
3. Specify in-class homework assignments
4. Identify what method will be used to evaluate student learning

What Research Backs It Up?

Data was gathered from ninety-three teachers over a period of two years. Data sources included individual and focus group interviews, written plans, and videotaped teaching episodes. In addition, focus group interviews with fifteen in-service and fifteen preservice teachers were conducted to obtain feedback about the utility of the planning pyramid.

IMPLEMENTING DIFFERENTIATED ASSESSMENT AND INSTRUCTION IN THE CLASSROOM

Standards must remain high and constant for all students, regardless of their academic readiness to work with a particular concept. The process of how it is achieved and how it may be demonstrated can vary from learner to learner, which is the basic premise of differentiated instruction. Whether students differ in interests, learning styles, or academic readiness, it is becoming ever more imperative that teachers be skilled and knowledgeable about how to meet learners' needs and allow them equal access to an education that supports them and thrives due to the differences they bring. It is no longer acceptable that students with varied academic levels are separated from their peers and put into separate categories for the gifted and talented, those with disabilities, and everyone else in between (Hess, 1999).

> *Standards must remain high and constant for all students, regardless of their academic readiness to work with a particular concept.*

In a differentiated classroom, a teacher is guided by the few key ideas that influence his or her approach to developing instruction that focuses on students' needs:

The components of teaching and learning are adjustable. Teaching and the tools used to teach can be different for the students in the classrooms; grouping of students can be flexible (whole class, individuals, or small groups), and demonstrating and assessing learning can vary.

Effective and continuous assessment should influence instruction. Teachers should use assessment in order to better understand the individual learner and determine instructional strategies that will most benefit that student. Assessment will ultimately influence the direction of instruction.

Students have access to activities that are equally interesting and challenging. Learning activities should focus on the same essential skills and knowledge for all students, but at the same time, an activity should be as challenging and interesting for the learner as another activity (using the same skills and knowledge) that is being offered to other students.

Teachers and students work together in the development of instruction and learning. Teachers should be challenging their learners by providing them opportunities to learn in ways that most benefit them. This learning occurs while the teacher facilitates the students' understanding through instruction that considers students' needs (Tomlinson & Allan, 2000).

TO SUM UP

This chapter provides two case studies of differentiated assessment in action and some research on use of a planning tool. The first case is from an urban public school, where Miguel selects work samples and creates portfolios for each student. Students reflect on their work during class on a weekly basis, using three key questions Miguel provides. He also begins each day with journal writing and later uses items in the journals as the basis for new lessons.

If students are struggling to write their thoughts, Miguel asks other students to volunteer to help, which is especially helpful for English language learners. He also lays out his classroom in a way conducive to observing students' work on their portfolios and to their being able to access information. He uses a lesson plan with multiple entry points, using ideas suggested by student work, and finds ways to let students use multiple intelligences. At the end of the year, each student compiles a "pass-along" portfolio that represents his or her progress for the school year.

The second case was a team of ninth-grade instructors who developed a differentiated lesson plan for an entire class using a planning pyramid with tiered assignments to differentiate what all students should learn from other learning that would be "nice to have" and that some students would be able to incorporate in their work. The author closes with research that backs up the use of the planning pyramid in a differentiated learning approach.

- The three key steps in the portfolio process are collecting work, selecting items that demonstrate growth, and reflecting on what these pieces demonstrate about the student and his or her learning.

- The physical environment must be constructed in a way that best lends itself to student assessment.

- Checklists can serve as a way to employ all eight intelligences in the classroom.

- The results of assessments should influence future instruction.

- All students should have access to activities that are interesting and challenging at their own levels.

- Students should be involved in the design of instruction and in how they are evaluated.

¿? DISCUSSION QUESTIONS

1. In what ways did Miguel accommodate cultural and linguistic differences in his classroom?

2. What methods does Miguel use to encourage students to reflect on their work as part of their daily routine?

3. How does Miguel's classroom reflect his use of sociocultural processes and engage multiple intelligences in his students?

4. In what ways is his teaching philosophy similar to yours? How is it different?

5. Even when you cannot control every aspect of the learning environment, what can you do that could help students learn in multiple ways?

6. What are some examples you know of teachers who develop lessons to accommodate cultural and linguistic differences? How do they do it?

7. How would you expect the lessons designed with the planning pyramid in Figure 7.6 to be different from other lessons? Why would differences exist?

8. In what ways can assignments be adapted for students with special needs? Give some examples.

9. In what ways can students be assessed taking their differences into account?

10. Discuss some ways in which students can be involved in planning lessons and designing assessments.

APPENDIX: DVD TABLE OF CONTENTS

Welcome to the DVD portion of this book. The following outline is intended to serve as a quick reference guide through the DVD. At the beginning of each DVD section, a short overview will provide a brief description of the contents for the given section. I hope you will use the materials in this DVD to not only supplement the book's text, but also to help you start generating your own ideas for incorporating digital portfolios into your classroom.

REFERENCES AND RESOURCES

Airasian, P. (1990). *Classroom assessment.* New York: McGraw-Hill.

Alvarez, M. D. (1991). Psychoeducational assessment of linguistic minority children: Current perspectives and future trends. In A. N. Amber (Ed.), *Bilingual education and English as a second language: A research handbook, 1988-90* (pp. 233–248). New York: Garland.

Ambert, A. N. (Ed.). (1991). *Bilingual education and English as a second language: A research handbook, 1988-90.* New York: Garland.

Andrade, H. G. (2000). Using rubrics to promote thinking and learning. *Educational Leadership, 57*(5), 13–18.

Andrade, H. G., et al. (September/October 2003). Role of rubric-referenced self-assessment in learning to write. *The Journal of Educational Research, 97*(1), 21–34.

Andrade, H. G. (Winter 2005). Teaching with rubrics: The good, the bad, and the ugly. *College Teaching, 53*(1), 27–30.

Baca, L., & Almanza, E. (1991). *Language minority students with disabilities.* Reston, VA: Council of Exceptional Children.

Baca, L.M., & Clark, C. (November 1992) *Exito: A Dynamic Team Assessment Approach for Culturally Diverse Students.* Paper presented at the Council of Exceptional Children. Minneapolis.

Barrett, H. C. (1998). Strategic questions: What to consider when planning for electronic portfolios. *Learning and Leading with Technology, 26*(2), 6–13.

Barrett, H. C. (2005). Researching electronic portfolios and learner engagement: The REFLECT Initiative. *Journal of Adolescent and Adult Literacy, 50*, 436–449.

Barrett, H. C. (March 2007). Researching electronic portfolios and learner engagement: The REFLECT Initiative. *Journal of Adolescent & Adult Literacy, 50*(6), 436–449.

Berger, S. L. (n.d.). Differentiating curriculum for gifted students. *ERIC Clearinghouse on Handicapped and Gifted Individual.* Retrieved March 19, 2002, from www.kidsource.com/kidsource/content/diff-curriculum.html.

Bolman, L., & Deal, T. (1994). *Becoming a teacher leader: From isolation to collaboration.* Thousand Oaks, CA: Corwin Press.

Classroom management and successful practices. (n.d.). Retrieved March 19, 2002, from www.mcps.k12.md.us/departments/eii/eiimanagepracticepage.html.

Corey, S. (1944, January). Poor scholar's soliloquy. *Childhood Education.*

Cummins, J. (1986). Empowering minority students: A framework for interventions. *Harvard Educational Review, 56*, 18–36.

Cummins, J. (1989). A theoretical framework for bilingual special education. *Exceptional Children, 65*, 111–119.

Damico, J. S. (1991). Descriptive assessment of communicative ability in limited English proficient children. In E. V. Hamayan & J. S. Damico (Eds.), *Limiting bias in the assessment of bilingual students.* Austin, TX: Pro-Ed.

Damico, J. S., et al. (November 1992). Descriptive assessment in the school meeting new challenges with new solutions. Paper presented at the Council of Exceptional Children, Minneapolis.

Darling-Hammond, L. (2010). *The flat world and education: How America's commitment to equity will determine our future.* New York: Teachers College Press.

DeLeon, J. (1990). A model for advocacy oriented assessment process in the psychoeducational evaluation of culturally and linguistically different students. *Journal of Issues of Linguistic Minority Students, 7*, 53–67.

Dolson, D. (1994). *Assessing students in bilingual contexts: Provisional guidelines.* Sacramento: California State Department of Education.

Drago-Severson, E. (2004). *Helping teachers learn: Principal leadership for adult growth and development.* Thousand Oaks, CA: Corwin Press.

Drago-Severson, E. (2004). *Helping teachers learn: Principal leadership for adult growth and development.* Thousand Oaks, CA: Corwin Press.

Edmonds, R. (1989). Good seeds grow in good cultures. *Educational Leadership, 52*, 45–58.

Fedoruk, G., & Norman, C. (1990). Kindergarten screening and predictive inaccuracy: First grade teachers' variability. *Exceptional Children, 57*, 258–263.

Fulk, A., & Mossburg, D. (n.d.). *Swimming upstream: Realities faced by students with learning disabilities in today's world.* Retrieved April 11, 2002, from http://www.1donline.org/mminds/fulk/mossburg.html.

Gardner, H. (1983). *Frames of mind: How children think and how schools should teach.* New York: Basic Books.

Gardner, H. (1993). *Multiple intelligences: The theory in practice.* New York: Basic Books.

Gardner, H. (1997). Multiple intelligences as a partner in school improvement. *Educational Leadership, 55*, 20–21.

Genessee, F., & Hamayan, E. (1994). Classroom based assessment. In F. Genessee (Ed.), *Education and second language children: The whole child, the whole curriculum, the whole community.* Cambridge: Cambridge University Press.

Genishi, C. (1992). *Ways of assessing children and curriculum: Stories of early childhood practice.* New York: Teachers College Press.

Gonzalez, V. (1998). *Assessment and instruction of linguistically diverse students with or at risk for learning problems: From research to practice.* Needham Heights, MA: Allyn and Bacon.

Goodrich, H. (1997). Understanding rubrics. *Educational Leadership, 54*, 14–17.

Hakuta, K., & Garcia, E. (1989). Bilingualism and education. *American Psychologist, 44*, 374–379.

Hamayan, E., & Damico, J. S. (1991). Developing and using a second language. In E. V. Hamayan & J. S. Damico (Eds.), *Limiting bias in the assessment of bilingual students* (pp. 35–75). Austin, TX: Pro-Ed.

Harris Stefanakis, E. (1994). *Preschool screening: Portfolio approach for linguistic minority individuals.* National Head Start Research. Translating Research into Practice. Arlington, VA.

Harris Stefanakis, E. (1997a). Portfolios: A way to sit beside the learner. In S. Veenema & S. Seidel (Eds.), *The Project Zero classroom.* Cambridge, MA: Project Zero Harvard Graduate School of Education.

Harris Stefanakis, E. (1997b). The power in portfolios: A way to sit beside the learner. In B. Torff (Ed.), *Multiple intelligences and assessment*. Palatine, IL: IRI Skylight.

Harris Stefanakis, E. (1998a). *What is it like for students to use their minds well in an urban high school?* Boston: Fenway Middle College High School.

Harris Stefanakis, E. (1998b). *Whose judgment counts? Assessing multilingual individuals (K-3).* Portsmouth, NH: Heinemann/Boynton Cook.

Harris Stefanakis, E. (1999). Teachers' judgments do count: Assessing multilingual students. In Z. Beykont (Ed.), *Lifting every voice: Pedagogy and politics of multilingualism* (pp. 139–160). Cambridge, MA: Harvard Education Publishing Group.

Harris Stefanakis, E. (2002). *Multiple intelligences and portfolios.* Portsmouth, NH: Heinemann.

Harris Stefanakis, E. (2003). *A portfolio resource guide for K-12 classroom educators (Greek and English).* Athens, Greece: Athens College Press.

Harris Stefanakis, E. (2006, January 8). Failing our students! *New York Times.*

Hernandez, R. (1994). Reducing bias in assessment of culturally and linguistically diverse populations. *Journal of Issues on Language Minority Students, 14*, 260–300.

Hess, M. A. (1999). *Teaching in mixed-ability classrooms.* Retrieved March 19, 2002, from www.weac.org/kids/1998-99/jmarch99/differ.htm.

Marshall, S. (1992). Managing the culture: The key to effective change. *School Organization, 13*, 255–268.

Menken, K. (2008). *English language learners left behind: Standardized testing as language policy.* New York: Multilingual Matters.

Munro, J. (2008). *Educational leadership.* New York: McGraw-Hill.

New York City, 2006. No retrieval date. http://schools.nyc.gov/default.htm.

Nunley, K. F. (n.d.-a). *Layered curriculum.* Retrieved April 11, 2002, from http://www.help4teachers.com/layeredcurriculum.htm.

Nunley, K. F. (n.d.-b). *Rubrics.* Retrieved April 11, 2002, from http://www.help4teachers.com/layeredcurriculum.htm.

Nunley, K. F. (n.d.-c). *Working with styles.* Retrieved April 11, 2002, from http://www.help4teachers.com/layeredcurriculum.htm.

Sadowski, M. (Ed.). (2004). *Teaching immigrant and second language students: Strategies for success.* Cambridge, MA: Harvard Education Press.

Saphier, J. (1993). *Activators: Activities to engage students' thinking before instruction.* Acton, MA: Research for Better Teaching.

Saphier, J., & King, M. (1985). Good seeds grow in strong cultures. *Educational Leadership, 42*(6), 67–74.

Schumm, J. S., & Vaughan, S. (1994). Planning pyramid: A framework for planning for diverse student needs during content area instruction. *Reading Teacher, 47*, 605–615.

Seidel, S. (1997). *Portfolio practices: Thinking through the assessment of children's work.* Washington, DC: National Education Association.

Snow, C. (1992). Perspectives on second language development: Implications for bilingual education. *Educational Researcher, 21*(2), 16–20.

TEDU student portfolio basics: Differentiated instruction. (n.d.). Retrieved March 19, 2002, from http://www.cedu.niu.edu/tedu/portfolio/diffclass.htm.

Tomlinson, C. A., and colleagues. (1995). *Differentiating instruction for advanced learners in the mixed-ability middle school classroom. ERIC Clearinghouse on Disabilities and Gifted Education.* Retrieved March 19, 2002, from http://www.ed-gov/databases/ERIC/digests/ed38914.html.

Tomlinson, C. A. (1999). *The differentiated classroom: Responding to the needs of all learners.* Alexandria, VA: Association for Supervision and Curriculum Development.

Tomlinson, C. A. (n.d.). *How can gifted students' needs be met in mixed-ability classrooms? Frequently asked questions.* Retrieved March 19, 2002, from http://www.bctf.ca.JPSAs/AEGTCCB/IRN/brochure.html.

Tomlinson, C. A., & Allan, S. D. (2000). *Leadership for differentiating schools and classrooms.* Alexandria, VA: Association for Supervision and Curriculum Development.

Tuttle, J. (2000, April). Differentiated classroom. *Woodbury Reports Archive,* 68. Retrieved March 19, 2002, from http://www.strugglingteens.com/archives/2004/oe04.html.

U.S. Census Bureau. (2006). American Community Survey. http://www.census.gov/.

Wagner, T. & Kegan, R. (2006). *Change leadership: A practical guide to transforming our schools.* San Francisco: John Wiley & Sons.

Wiggins, G. (1989). Teaching to the (authentic) test. *Educational Leadership, 46*(7), 41–47.

Wilkinson, C. (November 1992). *Curriculum based assessment.* Paper presented at the Council of Exceptional Children, Minneapolis.

Willis, S., & Mann, L. (2000). *Differentiating instruction: Finding manageable ways to meet individual needs.* Retrieved March 19, 2002, from http://www.ascd.org/readingroom/update/2000/1win.html.

Wolf, D. P. (1989). Portfolio assessment: Sampling student work. *Educational Leadership, 467*, 35–37.

INDEX

HOW TO USE THE DVD-ROM

SYSTEM REQUIREMENTS

PC with Microsoft Windows 2003 or later
Mac with Apple OS version 10.1 or later
It is necessary to have Quicktime installed in order for the videos to play.

USING THE DVD-ROM WITH WINDOWS

To view the items located on the DVD-ROM, follow these steps:

1. Insert the DVD-ROM into your computer's DVD-ROM drive.

2. A window appears with the following options:

   Contents: Allows you to view the files included on the DVD-ROM.

   Software: Allows you to install useful software from the DVD-ROM.

   Links: Displays a hyperlinked page of Web sites.

   Author: Displays a page with information about the author(s).

   Contact Us: Displays a page with information on contacting the publisher or author.

   Help: Displays a page with information on using the DVD-ROM.

   Exit: Closes the interface window.

If you do not have autorun enabled, or if the autorun window does not appear, follow these steps to access the DVD-ROM:

1. Click Start → Run.

2. In the dialog box that appears, type d:\start.exe, where d is the letter of your DVD-ROM-ROM drive. This brings up the autorun window described in the preceding set of steps.

3. Choose the desired option from the menu. (See step 2 in the preceding list for a description of these options.)

IN CASE OF TROUBLE

If you experience difficulty using the DVD-ROM, please follow these steps:

1. Make sure your hardware and systems configurations conform to the systems requirements noted under "System Requirements" above.

2. Review the installation procedure for your type of hardware and operating system. It is possible to reinstall the software if necessary.

To speak with someone in Product Technical Support, call 800-762-2974 or 317-572-3994 Monday through Friday from 8:30 A.M. to 5:00 P.M. EST. You can also contact Product Technical Support and get support information through our Web site at www.wiley.com/techsupport.

Before calling or writing, please have the following information available:

- Type of computer and operating system.

- Any error messages displayed.

- Complete description of the problem.

It is best if you are sitting at your computer when making the call.